SINGER ON THE SAND

SINGER ON THE SAND

The true story of an occurrence on the island
of Great Sangir, north of the Celebes,
more than a hundred years ago

by
Norma Youngberg

TEACH Services, Inc.
PUBLISHING
www.TEACHServices.com ● (800) 367-1844

Copyright © 1998, 2010 TEACH Services, Inc.
ISBN-13: 978-1-57258-142-5 (Paperback)
Library of Congress Control Number: 98-87349

TEACH Services, Inc.
P U B L I S H I N G
www.TEACHServices.com • (800) 367-1844

CHAPTER TOPICS

Chapter One

VISITORS

The sun had not yet risen above the hills of Great Sangir, but already the first bright light touched the volcano and tipped it with purple fire. The lower part of the smoking mountain still lay in shadow and its buttresses ran out into the ocean like the green, mossed-over roots of a giant stump, rotted away to a dull point.

The boy, Satoo, settled himself among the high rocks on the south side of the little bay that opened on the island's western shore. He puffed to catch his breath. He had run all the way from his father's house to see the sun rise on the fire mountain. The plumes of vapor that floated about its summit fascinated him, and from the safety of his rocky perch he often greeted the morning, watching the living color creep down the mountain as the light advanced, until the new day lay, like a blessing, around him.

The blue sea that stretched for a couple of miles between him and the fire mountain was smooth this morning, and only the faintest of breezes stirred the surface with ripples. The tide was out, and from the coral rocks below his hiding place the sharp smell of salt water and the damp sea floor came up to him. He breathed it in with eager joy, and it reminded him that the fish would be cooked for breakfast by now and he had better hurry home.

Then he saw the little interisland boat round the point of land that sheltered the bay from the southwest. The freight boat did not come often. Satoo stood up. He quivered all over with excitement. All thoughts of rushing home to breakfast vanished from his mind. The landing place was so close that he could stand right here and watch the unloading. Or, of course, he could run down to the landing place. He stood there among the rocks like a bird poised for flight. He had still not made up his mind.

Closer and closer the little ship came. Satoo saw the sailors ready the hawsers and lasso the huge wooden posts that stuck up out of the water at the jetty. The boy did not hesitate longer. He scrambled down from his lookout perch and ran to the landing place.

With a grinding noise of wood on wood, the boat slowly drew in to berth alongside the old wooden wharf.

During his twelve years of life Satoo had watched the freight boat dock and unload many times, but now he saw something on the deck of the ship that made his heart pound in his naked chest. He knew that this landing would not be like any he had seen before.

There were piles of curious-looking boxes stacked on the deck and there were people dressed in strange clothing—such a lot of clothing. He could see that they were not like any people he had ever seen before in all his life. There were four of them, a family, he guessed— a man, a woman, and two children. There was a boy about his own size and a little girl only a few years old.

"Who are they?" Satoo pointed a brown finger at the newcomers.

One of the sailors answered him. "They are teach ers. They have come from a country called Europe."

"Teachers! What are teachers?" Satoo stared at the queer long dresses the woman and the little girl wore. "Teachers ... teachers." He said the word over and over.

"You'll soon find out what teachers are." The sailor laughed. "They intend to live here, right here on this island of Great Sangir. They plan to teach you."

This disturbed Satoo for a moment. He had never heard of teachers and had no idea what they might intend to do to him. He couldn't imagine what kind of people they might be or what they might have in all those boxes and bundles, but he had no time to consider the matter any more at this time. The boxes were coming off the boat as the teacher told the men how to handle them and where to put them.

Although this man was bigger than any person Satoo had ever seen before, the boy didn't feel afraid of him. His eyes were of a strange light color, but they were deep-set, large, and happy-looking. Long red hair bushed out from his face. Satoo supposed that the hair of his head must be the same color, but the man wore a thick sun helmet and no one could see his hair. The big man wore long pants that came down to his feet, and his feet looked black and hard, with no toes at all. He wore a light-colored jacket.

Satoo turned to look at the boy. He had eyes like his father and a shock of reddish-yellow hair. It was the brightest hair that Satoo had ever seen—brighter even than the feathers of any island bird. Now what could be the meaning of such a head of hair? How could it have grown out of this boy's head? He must have used strong witch medicine to make it come out that color.

The little girl's hair was light colored too, but not so bright as the boy's. The children's mother wore a cloth of pale blue around her head, so Satoo couldn't tell whether she had any hair. She wore a long dress that reached almost to her feet. Then he saw that her feet were not bare like the island women's. Both of them were cased up in some strange-looking things, black and shiny. He looked at the man's feet again, and decided that his feet were not naturally black and hard. They were thrust into those cases too, but both the children were barefoot.

Satoo lifted his face to the downpour. The cool rain felt good on his skin. Then he saw the big man under the cloth, beckoning him to come.

As the teacher stacked his boxes in a neat pile on the beach behind the landing platform, Satoo glanced up at the sky. He knew it would soon rain. During this season it rained every day at this time.

"Scurry around, you fellows." The captain of the boat spoke to his men. "Get all the teacher's stuff into that pile and cover it. Can't you see the rain is coming? Hurry, they will get wet."

The big man seemed to understand what the captain had said. He waved the remark aside with his hand and stooped to open one of his packages. He shook out an enormous piece of thick cloth and threw it over the heap of baggage. Then he weighted each of the four corners with a stone. While everyone else scurried back onto the boat and sheltered under its foredeck, the teacher waited for the first sharp flurry of raindrops. Then he lifted one corner of the gray cloth and crouched there with his boxes, holding the cover over him like a leaf.

Satoo hadn't moved. He cared nothing for the rain. He wore only a loincloth made of bark, and it dried easily. The cool rain felt good on his skin and he lifted his face to the downpour. Then he saw the big man under the gray cloth beckon him to come. The man pointed to the shelter where he crouched and invited Satoo to join him and share it.

Suddenly Satoo felt afraid. Chills chased each other up and down his back. He turned and pelted home through the rain. Faster and faster he ran until he burst into his father's hut, where the family were just finishing breakfast.

"Where have you been?" his mother asked. "We called and called. What were you doing?"

"There's a boat!" Satoo gasped out the words. "It has just come, and there are strange people on it."

He threw himself on the matted floor beside his father, Chief Meradin. The chief sat for a moment and looked at his son.

Then he looked down again at his banana-leaf plate. He dipped up his fish and taro with a steady hand. "How many of the strange people are there?"

"Just a big man, a woman, and two children."

"Well, if there are no more than that, we needn't be afraid. We can easily manage so few."

"Come now, eat your breakfast." Satoo's mother handed him a leaf plate piled with food.

The drip, drip of the rain beat on the thatched roof with a muffled sound. The pigs under the house grunted, squealed, and fought with one another as they crowded away from the driving rain. Satoo looked out the open door of the hut and saw the grove of coconut trees bend before the stiff wind.

"The man is sitting over there at the landing place under a big piece of cloth. It is so large it covers all his boxes. He has a great pile of things he has brought along."

"Trade goods," the chief muttered between bites of food. "Merchandise..."

"No, no, I'm sure it isn't." Satoo finished his last gulp of taro and wadded the green leaf that had been his plate. "I'm sure. You see, the captain of the boat was very polite to him, and one of the sailors told me that this man is a teacher and he intends to stay here, to live here. What is a teacher, Father?"

The chief stopped eating and ran his hands through his thick curly hair. He got to his feet and looked out the open door toward the landing place. "A teacher?...A teacher? And they plan to stay here?"

"The sailor told me they would." Satoo came to stand beside his father in the door. Together they gazed out into the heavy shower. The rain beat down in sheets, and it was impossible to see anything so far away as the boat landing.

"Where will they stay?" Satoo studied his father's face.

"I think I'd better go and see about this." The chief dashed out into the rain and Satoo followed him.

They had run half the way down the path before they could see the landing place. Then the shower stopped suddenly and the sun shone down hot on the wet sand. The clouds rolled away in the bright blue heaven. The daily rain was over. They could see that the captain of the freight boat had loosened his hawsers from the wooden posts and was pulling out into the surf.

By the time the chief and Satoo puffed breathlessly up to the little group at the landing place, the ship was beyond the hail of a human voice.

In spite of the rain a number of the village people had already gathered. The teacher opened a package and distributed small sweet cakes and lumps of sugar to everyone.

When the teacher saw Chief Meradin he smiled down at him and offered him and Satoo cakes and sugar. The man appeared to be friendly, no doubt of that, and he had a rich full voice that was not one thread of sound, but many threads woven together.

Satoo wondered whether the teacher knew that his father was the chief of this village. Could he know that the big figure of a fish tattooed on his chest and those magnificent earrings of carved teeth could be worn only by chiefs of the islands?

Yes, the teacher looked at the chief and motioned toward his boxes and packages. He pointed in the direction of the village among the coconut trees on the rising ground to the north. He waited for the chief to make some motion of welcome. But Satoo saw that his father was puzzled and could not think what to do. If the boat was still here he could ask the captain to take the strange people away, and that would settle everything, but the boat was now far out in the choppy ocean. No one knew when it might return. It might be weeks.

The strange woman and the children sat on the pile of boxes. They laughed and smiled and acted as friendly as the big man. Again Satoo looked at the boy's hair and marveled at its brightness.

Hans, Hans," the teacher spoke to his son. "Hans," he said again as he took the boy's hand and pulled him off the box. He led him to Satoo. The red-haired boy took Satoo's hand in his and held it firmly. Again the teacher said, "Hans."

Satoo looked into the boy's blue eyes. He knew now that this boy's name was Hans. The boy smiled and Satoo smiled back. The boy ran and brought his little sister and made Satoo and his father understand that her name was Marta. The little girl took hold of Satoo's hand. Her two long yellow braids jumped up and down as she danced about the two boys laughing and chattering in a language the people of Sangir had never heard before.

Again the teacher pointed to his baggage and then to the path that led up to the village. Satoo knew what he meant. He wanted them all to help him carry the things to the village, and he wanted someone to show him a place where they might stay.

Satoo saw his father's face darken into a frown. He knew that his father feared these smiling people, yet he must decide something about them.

"We will put them in Tama's hut." The chief finally spoke to old Gola, one of the village men who stood near him. "The hut leaks, but it can be fixed with a few handfuls of grass. Tama is over on the other side of the island and he isn't likely to come back for several days."

Satoo caught his breath. Tama was the village witch doctor. Perhaps the magic of the new teachers and Tama's familiar spirits might not agree. It was a daring thing for Chief Meradin to put these people in Tama's house. Certainly Tama would not be pleased. Satoo was sure the witch doctor would not welcome these people to the island, although he didn't know yet just what a teacher might be. But of course father had a right to do anything he wanted. After all, he was the village chief.

The men and women shouldered the big and little packages and boxes and the procession trotted up along the beach path toward the village. Satoo carried a bundle on his head and Hans carried one too. The boys ran along together, and they both laughed because Satoo carried his bundle on his head as easily as he carried his hair, but Hans kept dropping his. Satoo thought that bright hair might have something to do with it, but he could only laugh about it. Conversation was limited.

Satoo was surprised to see that the white woman and the little girl, Marta, didn't carry anything. He thought this a strange thing, because the women of Sangir always worked more than the men. They carried the heaviest loads and did the hardest work.

By the time they stood in front of Tama's hut the sun had risen to the midheaven. Satoo put down his package and looked back toward the bay and the great fire mountain, where it stood up out of the sea like the stump of a mighty tree that might have reached to the heaven of stars had it not been cut down a long time ago.

Chapter Two

CHUNKS OF MAGIC

When the sun went down behind the fire mountain in a blaze of rose and gold and violet light, Satoo left his father's house and walked the few rods to the hut where the family of strange people must be getting settled for the night, their first night on Sangir. Their first night in the witchman's hut.

All day long the village people had stood around in curious groups watching the bearded man pry open boxes and arrange beds for his family. They all knew now that his hair was as red and curly as his beard. The people even pressed close to the door and watched the family eat, which was rude, of course, but all the village folk excused themselves to one another, because this was such an unusual occasion and such a queer sight. They just couldn't take their fascinated gaze away from those eating tools these people used. They ate from strange dishes too, not from bowls of coconut shells or green leaves from the jungle, although there was an abundant supply of fine large leaves there in the edge of the jungle a few yards away, between the village and the sea.

Satoo peeked with the others. The thatch walls of Tama's house were loose and full of holes. There were many places where an eye could be pressed close and see plenty. If there was no opening at the right level, one could easily be poked through.

If the people inside the house knew how many on-lookers watched their movements, they did not appear to give it a thought. They unpacked some of their goods; other boxes they stored, unopened, in one corner of the hut. It was of one room only and about twelve by twenty feet in size, with an earthen cooking place on the floor in one end. It was small, for the witchman, Tama, lived there alone. He had neither wife nor child, nor even an animal to keep him company.

Out of one box Satoo saw the teacher take several squarish-looking things that opened at one side, and the boy was astonished to see that the objects were not solid. They were made of thin leaves, one on top of another. This amazing sight drew exclamations of fear and surprise from all the people who manned the peep-holes, as well as from those who stood in the door of the witchman's hut.

"Magic," they whispered to one another. "What a lot of magic this strange man has brought."

Most of the squarish-looking things were brown or black, and they were not all the same size or thickness. The teacher handled them with care, as though they were precious to him.

"Yes, it is magic." One of the village men spoke to Satoo. "We might have known that he would bring magic with him, but I didn't expect it to look like that. Of course all people use their own kind. No one can live without magic."

Full of fear and wonder the villagers went home. It was dark now, and it was not prudent to stay longer near the hut where the new teacher was unpacking such strange-looking magic.

"I think it is a dangerous thing for those people to sleep in Tama's hut," Satoo told his mother. "That is the place where Tama talks to his devils. What if the two kinds of magic begin to fight each other?"

"Don't worry about it," mother said. "How do we know that Tama didn't take his devils along with him? He usually does. He will need them all, over on the other side of the island."

But Satoo could see that most of the village people worried about it, for they shut their doors early, barred them, and went to their sleeping mats.

Satoo's curiosity about the new family would not let him rest. His interest overcame his fear, and he left his sleeping mat, crawled to the door, let himself out; and in the light of the rising moon, he crossed over to Tama's hut and fastened his eyes to a peephole at the back side of the hut nearest the jungle.

The room inside looked rather neat already. The teacher and his wife and Hans and the little girl, Marta, were sitting quietly on some of the boxes they had opened and turned upside down. The teacher held one of the chunks of magic in his hands, and he looked right inside the strange thing and talked to it. Would the chunk of magic talk back?

Satoo's heart quickened at this sight and tingles ran along his spine. He resisted a strong urge to run home, and he did take his eye from the peephole in the matting for just an instant to throw an apprehensive glance at the dark jungle behind him.

Then he looked again. The big teacher was still talking to the black thing. Once in a while he looked up at his wife and children, then went on speaking to the magic again.

"It must be some kind of spirit that lives in there," Satoo told himself. The thought frightened him so much that he would surely have run away, but now the man closed up the box of magic and laid it on his knees. Then he opened his mouth and began to sing.

Satoo knew what singing was. He had heard the dancing tunes of his village all his life and he had heard the monotonous chants of Tama, the witch doctor, but the sounds that came out of this big teacher's mouth were different from anything the island boy had ever heard or imagined. They were bright tingling bands of melody woven into a pattern of such sweetness and beauty that tears filled Satoo's eyes. Then, again, terrible fear struck him. This must be the magic the man had drawn from the boxlike thing. He could easily become bewitched if he stayed and listened to it. Perhaps he was already bewitched.

Then he saw that the village people were stealing out of their houses and creeping toward Tama's little tumbledown hut, where the lovely sounds swelled and filled the night.

The people came in twos and threes and in companies. They didn't try to peek through the walls. They stood a few feet away from the walls of the hut and listened while the glorious notes swung up and out, floated and fluttered, and soared away into heights of joy where none of them could follow. And over the strange scene the moon climbed the sky as it brightened and flooded the village with light.

No one spoke, but as the rhythm of the song possessed them they began to sway to the cadence of the song, and at every pause a breathed "Ah-h-h-!" wafted up from the circle of people.

When the singing at last ended, they stole back to their houses. Satoo lay on his mat for a long time thinking about what he had seen, and the delicious music of the teacher's voice still flowed through his body like a rich river of happiness. But he dare not let himself be happy. This had all come out of that boxlike thing, and no doubt it was the most dangerous kind of magic. He wished that Tama would hurry back. Tama would know how to handle this new witchcraft. With these thoughts in his mind, Satoo slept at last.

Singing waked Satoo on the following morning. That teacher must love to sing and that chunk of magic must be full of it. And from that day forward, so long as the big teacher and his family stayed in Tama's house, the people heard songs in the morning and songs at night.

The songs were not always the same, and this bewildered Satoo, because, again and again, he tried to make such sounds come out of his own throat, but they always sounded like the thin cry of a wounded bird or the pitiful bleat of a goat.

Even the teacher's little daughter could sing, and this surprised Satoo more than anything else. Often the big man put his little child on his knees and they sang to each other in the same rich surge of melody. Little Marta's voice was sweet and as true as her father's.

The very first day after his landing the teacher began walking about the village area looking here and there and measuring with his eyes and testing the soil with the toe of his black-booted foot.

"I know what he is looking for," Chief Meradin told his family. "He is looking for a place to build his own house. With all the stuff he brought he needs a larger place."

Satoo saw the scowl darken his father's face. The boy knew that his father wished that the teacher had never come to Great Sangir. It was a perplexing problem to know what to do with this family, but they were here now and something must be decided.

By signs and gestures and foreign words the teacher tried to make the chief understand that he wanted some land where he might build his house, but the chief always shook his head. No matter how many times the big man led Chief Meradin to some vacant spot and showed him with a stick how large a piece of land he wanted, the chief always shook his head.

"He will go away," the chief said. "When he doesn't find any place to build his house he will go away. Someday the freight boat will come back and then he will go. Even a bird will not stay where it cannot build a nest."

But the chief was wrong. The freight boat came and left, and still the big teacher went every day to different places on the island, always to be refused even the smallest piece of land.

Satoo could see that his father was more worried than ever, because now some of the village people were so pleased with the big man's kind ways and his beautiful songs that they whispered to one another that Chief Meradin was doing a bad thing to refuse even a small plot of ground, for there was plenty of vacant garden land near the village.

It had been a number of days since the freight boat's visit when the big teacher took his son, Hans, and went into the jungle between the village and the seashore. That afternoon they dragged out a few timbers and poles. The whole village watched them pull them over to a spot on the sand. After that the two of them went into the jungle almost every day, and the heap of materials on the beach grew to be a big pile.

"Do you suppose he is going to make his house right down there on the sand, on the salt grass?" Chief Meradin looked vexed. "Nothing will grow there, and no one can build a good house on the sand. It isn't solid."

As the days passed, it became clear to everyone that the teacher intended to build his house on the beach. It also became clear that it was a good and profitable thing to help him with the building. When some of the friendly village folk offered to help him cut the logs and bring them from the jungle he rewarded them with presents. More and more people came to help. They cut and trimmed the timbers, and the house on the beach grew much faster than Chief Meradin liked. Some of the women valued the pretty red and blue cloth that the teacher's wife gave them, and they wove grass matting for the walls and tied thatch for the roof. In fact, it was not many days until the house on the sand stood up proud and new beside the blue ocean and right across from the fire mountain. It stood above the high-tide mark and back a few yards on the level salt grass.

One morning Satoo came down to the new house, as he did every day. He overtook Hans, who was carrying a big flat stone from the beach.

"What are you doing?" he asked the red-haired boy.

"Come, help me." Hans put the stone on a pile beside the new house. "Come, we need many stones."

Hans did not yet know many words of the island language but the ones he knew were important and he used them every day. As Satoo worked with him, bringing more stones from the beach, the two boys spoke to each other in sign language, together with the few words they both knew.

"What for? What for?" Satoo tried to make his native language simple enough so Hans could understand.

For answer Hans pointed to his father, who had come out of the new house and stood looking at the pile of stones with a broad smile on his face. Satoo could see that for some reason the stones pleased the big teacher. Then the man rolled up the sleeves of his thin jacket and began to carry the stones nearer the house. Satoo watched him bring soft mud from higher up on the slope where the rich garden land began. Then the boy saw that the teacher intended to build a deep trough with the stones. He built it close against the walls of the house, so it looked as though the house grew right out of the stone trough.

Satoo was so curious that he could hardly wait to know what the trough was for, and he grew impatient with Hans, who did not know enough words to explain to him.

"Wait, wait, you will see," Hans told him. And Satoo had to wait. Other village people came and carried stones, and it took them more than one day. Several days had passed before the trough was finished all the way around the house. It was about two and a half feet deep and as wide across. When it was all done the big teacher led the village people into the jungle, where they filled baskets with rich leaf mold and moist soil. They carried it to the beach ad filled the trough around the teacher's house.

Then the big man showed the people some seeds. Satoo understood now. The teacher could not have a garden because nothing would grow on the salt grass. Chief Meradin had refused to give him any of the garden land that sloped tip to the hill above the beach. So the teacher would make a garden in the stone trough.

Chief Meradin came to look. "This teacher has a strong heart," he said. "It must be the magic that comes out of those black things."

Satoo was so interested in the seeds the teacher had planted that he went several times a day to see if they had sprouted. When they did come through the soil they were so tiny it was almost impossible to tell that they were really plants. But in a few days round leaves appeared, and when the boy bent over to examine them, a strong and pleasant fragrance came from the leaves.

By the time the plants in the stone trough had grown as high as Satoo's chest and clusters of red flowers had begun to form on them, the teacher had learned to speak many words in the language of Sangir. Also he had whitewashed his house and the stones of the outside wall of the trough. It looked beautiful there on the green salt grass with its white walls and its garden of green plants and red blossoms clustered about it.

The teacher also built a low fence of rocks around a small plot of ground surrounding the house; so it stood in the midst of a salt-grass lawn with the low stone wall enclosing it. He whitewashed the wall, too. When the rains washed the whitewash off, he brushed it on again and again.

With the help of some village men the big teacher built a boat too. It was a good boat, but not like any of the other island boats, because the teacher put something on it that made it white like his house. The island people soon discovered that the red-haired man was a good fisherman.

Chief Meradin watched the building of the house on the beach and said little, but Satoo knew that his father was greatly troubled. Of course everyone knew that the chief would not molest the teacher in his new house on the sand. The sand belonged to no one. It was the property of the sea spirits.

The chief could not keep the village people from visiting the teacher's house or from eating the sweet little cakes the teacher's wife baked in her stone oven, or from listening to the teacher and his family when they sang the lovely songs at sunrise and sundown.

"I just don't know what to do," the chief finally said one day. "I think I must call Tama back from the other side of the island. He has been away for many weeks now. He will know how to fight this witchcraft."

Satoo saw the messenger start off up the hill to carry the chief's word to Tama, and his heart felt heavy. He knew that trouble was coming. The old witchcraft and the new would never mix.

Chapter Three

TAMA, THE WITCHMAN

Tama, the witchman, was in the midst of a spirit feast when Chief Meradin's messenger reached him. For three days he had fasted, and now he sat among his charms and beat upon his spirit gourd. Around him the village people danced and chanted, and before him lay several sick persons.

There was much stomach sickness at this season on this side of the island, and the people had sent for him to come and cast out the devils that caused the trouble.

"There is a big red-haired teacher who has come to our village," the messenger told Tama. "He tried to get the chief to give him land among the village houses, but of course he wouldn't do it. The chief hoped he would go away, but what do you think he has done? He has built a new house right on the sea sand."

The messenger sat down on the ground. The dancing people stopped whirling and looked at him. Tama sat among his charms and considered this news. "Yes, I heard about this already," he said. "Why didn't the chief send him away?"

"He would surely have done it when the boat came back, if he had known how things would turn out; but now it is too late. Many of the village people have been taken in the heart by the teacher's magic. They go to his house every day, and even the chief's son, Satoo, follows these people like he had been born into their family."

Tama still sat cross-legged among his roots and bones and strong mixtures of herbs. He thought for a long time about what the messenger had said. Then he stood up and shook himself.

"Chief Meradin has sent for me. I must go." He began to gather up his things.

"Ah, do not leave us now," some of the people begged. "The sickness is beginning to slacken. Stay just a little longer and we shall be rid of it."

"There is a worse sickness back in my own village." Tama spoke in a sorrowful voice. "Sickness of the heart is always worse than sickness of the body."

"Go," Tama commanded the messenger, who still sat on the ground. "Go at once and tell the chief that I will come. I will start today."

The messenger hurried away and Tama continued to collect his things. When he had packed them all in a neat bundle he went to take his mat and rice pot from the house where he had slept. Then he turned his steps down the jungle path toward his own village on the opposite side of the island. As he walked he meditated on what could be done about this problem of the strange teacher.

Tama had heard of these foreign people who called themselves teachers. Some of them had visited the big island to the south. He knew what they had done there. He knew what they intended to do here. Their purpose was to change the old customs. There would be no more wild feasts with drinking and devil dances and secret magic performances.

The witch doctor knew that these teachers disapproved of such things, because they worshipped one great Spirit. He heard that they got their magic out of square, flat boxes. This magic could be fed to people through words, and the people who swallowed it came to enjoy it more than feasts or dancing or anything else. It was a terrible thing. The more Tama thought about it, the more he worried, and the anger inside him swelled and burned.

Tama marked the lighted window and the open door of the teacher's house and sat down on the salt grass outside the low white wall.

He decided that he would not stop at any village or house along the way. He would not eat, although he had already fasted for three days. He would not speak to any one. He would call all his familiar spirits and ask them to descend with him on his own village, and he would make a great attack on this teacher and rid the place of him and his magic.

All through the afternoon he walked, and when night came he slept in the jungle. With the first faint glow of the sunrise he was up again, and mile after weary mile he climbed and plodded his way toward the village of Chief Meradin. Now he began to blame himself because he had not hurried home when he first heard the news of these strangers. He had been a fool to stay away. He might have known something like this would happen— even the chief's son, Satoo. And he had such good plans for Satoo, planned to make him a witch doctor. The boy was bright and full of ideas. Now...

It was already evening when Tama entered his own village. The people must have finished bathing and eating by now. They would all be shut in their houses and, yes, they must be asleep already. Every hut was dark.

Then Tama saw a light far out on the beach where no light had ever been before. It must be the teacher's house on the sand. In spite of the heavy load he carried, his empty stomach, and his aching back, he swung around so he could inspect the house.

He couldn't see it very well in the dark, but he marked the lighted windows and the open door. The house was full of people—his own village people. At this instant a burst of sound came from the little house. It startled Tama. He staggered back and sat down on the salt grass outside the low white wall that loomed before him. He could see it in the faint moonlight.

The song rose and swelled, and the mighty voice of the teacher crashed into his mind like a troop of enemy warriors. He knew that he should hurry to his own hut. He should go at once to tell Chief Meradin that he was home now, and would do battle with this new witchcraft; but he could not rise from the spot where he had fallen. The music had struck him down like a hand. Now it grew. It soared like a bird and thundered like mighty waves. Over and over it rose and fell around him and the night and the whole world trembled with it. Tama lay helpless and shaking on the salt grass. Then the song stopped.

The witchman leaped to his feet, grabbed his bundles and his sleeping mat, and raced for his hut in the village. He pushed in the door, threw his things down, and squatted among them all out of breath and overcome with weariness, hunger, and fear.

As he sat in the dark hut he could hear the village folks coming back up to their houses. Their voices sounded unusually happy. They sang snatches of the song they had heard in the teacher's house and chattered in gay voices.

Tama listened with anger rising inside him like a flashing fire, but he neither moved nor spoke. When the sounds died away he got up and lighted his coconut-oil lamp. Then he began to sniff the air. A peculiar odor filled the hut. Now he realized that he had smelled it ever since he came in. He opened the door wider, and propped it. He threw open the one window at the back of the hut, but the smell persisted. Then he looked around. He found a pile of dry wood beside his cooking place. The clay fireplace had been brushed and cleaned of all ashes. Even the stones looked as if they had been scoured. Tama began to shake with fear. He laid some of the dry twigs among the stones of the fireplace and lighted a bit of wood fuzz with a spark from his spear and a flint stone that he carried in his pack. The fuzz smoked and flamed; the twigs caught and fire flared up in the empty room.

The witchman stared about the place and wondered whether this could possibly be the hut he had left a few weeks before. It was clean and fresh, as though every thing in it was newly washed. The floor was scrubbed, the walls were scrubbed, the low flat stool along the wall was scrubbed, and some bright shells lay there. One of the larger shells held a few wildflowers.

Tama got down on his hands and knees. He smelled of the shells, of the floor, and the clean matting that made the walls. The smell was all over. It came from everything. It must be something they had used to wash all these things.

And who were "they"? Someone had used this hut while he was gone. It couldn't be... but it must be! The chief must have let the new teacher and his family stay here until the man could get his new house built on the sand.

Tama gave the hut a thorough search. He found food ready for his use; some kinds of food he had never seen before. He put it all away, took some cassava from his own stores, and began to prepare his supper. He must have food now. He must have strength.

As the firelight played about the room and Tama began to feel rested and warmer, he noticed other things. The roof was mended. He saw that the walls had been repaired. Then he looked at the floor and saw that it had been renewed in all the weak worn places and was now as solid as when the hut was newly built.

"This magic is strong," he said to himself, and began to eat his first meal in several days.

He had scarcely lifted the first mouthful when he heard the chief's voice calling outside the hut. "You are home, Tama?"

Tama went to the open door. "I am home," he said into the darkness, and Chief Meradin came up the little ladder into the hut and sat down on a mat.

"They stayed here?" Tama swept his hand around the room as though to indicate that the strangers had stayed all over the hut, in every crevice and strand of it.

"Yes, there was no other place to put them." The chief looked so troubled that Tama felt sorry for him.

"And you thought the spirits might bother them if you put them here?"

The chief nodded. Tama offered him food, and they began to eat together.

"Yes," the chief said. "I hoped that the spirits living here might make them sick or at least worry them until they would decide to go away when the freight boat should return next time."

"It didn't work? It was no use?"

"No, it didn't work." Chief Meradin looked dejected. "They have strong magic. Even in his voice the big teacher has strong magic." He leaned forward and spoke in a lower voice. "You know, I think all the devils around here rushed away into the jungle. It is a great thing to hear—that singing."

"Yes, I should think so." Tama bent over his leaf plate, but he didn't tell the chief that he had listened to the singing this very evening and had felt its power.

Chief Meradin ate in silence for a long time until he had finished the food and crumpled the leaf he used for a plate. Then he leaned forward again and put his two brown hands together with all the finger tips touching.

"Now, it's like this." He spoke in an earnest tone. "We will have to do something or all the people in this village will follow the big teacher. They go every day to listen to his magic, and you know as well as I, that means the end of feasts and devil dancing. There will be no more drinking. There'll be no fun any more."

"It looks like the people are ready for some new thing." Tama threw out the crumpled leaves they had used as plates and brushed the crumbs down through the cracks in the bamboo floor.

The chief had not spoken. He sat with one hand on his forehead as though he worried and grieved. Tama sat down beside him.

"I have thought about this problem all the long journey back over the hills, and here's how it looks to me. Since the village people are bent on having some new teaching, why don't we ask the Islam teachers to bring their magic here? They will not interfere with the devil dances or the feasts or any of the good old customs. Of course they will require us to pray to Allah, but since we already spend a lot of time praying to the spirits, it will not be much trouble to pray to Allah too."

The chief thought about this for a long time. He sat there on the mat and scratched his head and frowned.

Finally he spoke. "I suppose you are right, Tama. I wish there was some other way, but I guess there isn't. This thing is already too big for us to fight alone. We must bring in some strong new magic. Yes, I'm sure you are right."

"I see that the teacher has built his house right down there on the sand." Tama stood up and looked out the door to see if there might be a light still shining in the teacher's house, but the beach was dark.

"The teacher begged me for land, all over the village and back into the hills, but of course I wouldn't let him have any." The chief came to stand beside Tama in the door.

"Does it seem to you that the fire mountain blows out more fire than usual tonight?" Tama asked.

"Ever since those teachers came it has rumbled and thundered and spewed out smoke and fire almost all the time. What do you think?"

"You know what I think. The fire spirits are angry about this new magic," Tama said. "Can't the village people see that it is so? Don't they know that it's dangerous to run after foreign magic?"

Neither man spoke for a long time. The volcano belched its fire against the night sky. The solid ground trembled. The hiss of the sea as the fiery rocks spilled over into it and the deep thunder that shuddered under the earth awed them both, but at last they turned back to the lamp-lighted room. They had seen the volcano active all their lives, and it was only a little worse than usual. They sat down again and began to plan for the Islam teachers whom they intended to invite to Great Sangir.

Chapter Four

MARTA

The witch doctor and Chief Meradin sat in the hut where Tama lived. It was evening of the day after Tama returned to his village tired and hungry and full of anger because of the new magic the big teacher had brought to the island of Great Sangir. The two men sat and talked about what could be done to rid the village of the teacher's family. Over and over they came back to Tama's suggestion that the only thing, the only plan, that held any promise, was to bring Islam teachers from the southern islands and encourage the people to follow the customs of Islam.

"Now when the new teachers come," Tama advised the chief, "you must give them the good garden land right behind the teacher's house. You know how it slopes up the hill there. But it is not too steep and it is rich. Anything will grow there."

Tama felt better than he had since he left the village on the other side of the island. His stomach was full again and the chief agreed to his plan.

"I will see that the Islam teachers have a fine new house, and they can plant all sorts of vegetables and fruit trees. They will prosper because you and I will see to it that they get the best of everything." The chief's voice sounded cheerful again.

"I'm sure this is the best way—the only way. Little by little the people will see that Islam is best, because it will not take away our old customs."

When Chief Meradin left Tama's hut he stood tall and strong, and the witchman knew that he would lose no time in carrying out the plans they had made.

Marta came into Tama's hut, carrying a bunch of red flowers that she handed to the witch doctor with a smile. He knelt to receive it.

Tama unrolled his sleeping mat and stretched out on it. He was so tired from his long walk across the island that he ached in every joint. Then it began to rain, and he thought wearily that now he must get up and move his mat because it was right under the bad place in the roof. Then he remembered.... The roof was mended. He settled back on his mat with deep satisfaction.

"Now why did the teacher mend my leaky roof?" Tama asked himself. "I wouldn't have done it."

He remembered that the hut where he had slept on the other side of the island had a big hole in its roof and he had never thought of mending it.

Tama slept well, for he was tired, and also a big load had been lifted from his mind since the chief had agreed to his plan about the Islam teachers.

The sun had already risen when he wakened the next morning, and as he went down to bathe he saw people coming and going between the village and the teacher's house on the beach.

There were two springs in the village, one in the jungle a little way back of Tama's hut and another near the center of the village. The people used both of them, but the one in the center of the village was larger, and the women gathered there to gossip and bathe, so the men often used the jungle spring. Tama always used it unless there was some special news he wanted to gather or some village problem that he knew would be talked about at the village spring.

After his bath Tama walked down the beach to get a look at the teacher's house by daylight. The whiteness of everything astonished him. When he saw the green plants growing around the house in their trough of whitewashed stones he drew in his breath with a sharp whistle.

Then he heard a noise. He looked toward the lower beach and saw a boy with flaming red hair. This must be the teacher's son. No one had told him about this boy. The witch doctor could only stare at such bright hair and marvel at how it could have grown out of a human head. The red-haired boy was not alone. The chief's son, Satoo, was with him. The two scurried off among the coral rocks chattering and gesturing after the manner of boys who are best friends.

"Not a bit too soon, not a bit too soon," Tama muttered to himself as he walked back to his hut.

He cooked his breakfast and threw out the soiled leaves he used for plates. Then he saw something that widened his eyes with surprise and made him lay his hand across his pounding heart. A small girl child was coming toward his open door. She wore a long pink dress that fluttered in the wind. Her shining yellow hair hung in two fat braids down her back. Her face was round and sweet and her eyes the blue color of sky on a cloudless day.

The child must belong to the big teacher, but what was she doing here? She did not pause but came right up the ladder and into Tama's hut. She did not act surprised to see him. She carried a little bunch of red flowers. She held them out to him and smiled.

The child was beautiful. Tama looked at her with a feeling in his chest that was almost an ache. He knelt on the floor and took the blossoms from her little white hand. He touched the small fingers, and they felt warm and moist. He took the little hand in his, and the child laughed and spoke words he could not understand. Then she pulled her hand away, ran for the broom, made of coconut fibers, and whisked it into every corner of the room, brushing and sweeping with painstaking care. Then she went to the fireplace and lifted the cooking pot. Tama watched her from the back window as she
38

lugged the heavy kettle to the jungle spring, scoured it with sand, and washed it clean in the flowing water. Then she carried it back up the ladder and set it upside down beside the cooking place. All the time she worked she sang a soft little song to herself.

"She is like a bird, a small pink bird," the witchman said to himself. "She works and sings, but I'm sure her father and mother don't know that I am home. They would never let her come here if they knew."

When her work was finished and the hut swept clean and every speck of ashes brushed from the clay stove, the child looked out the open door toward her own house on the beach. She started to go down the ladder, then came back and held out both hands to Tama. She smiled, and her blue eyes danced as she tried to make him understand words of her queer language. Then she hurried down the ladder and ran along the path to the beach and home.

Tama watched her until she went into the door of her own house; then he turned back to the empty hut. The day had suddenly darkened. Was the morning rain coming so soon? He looked out the door again, but not a cloud floated across the blue heaven.

The witchman sat down in his clean hut and began to store away the charms and medicines from his pack. He sorted the bundles of roots and herbs. He polished the bones and teeth. One of his clusters of slick black seeds had broken apart, and he spent the middle part of the day braiding new strings to hold the charms.

As he worked he thought of the little child. She was different from any child he had ever seen before. No island girl ever had such eyes and hair, but it wasn't that, either...no, it wasn't her looks. After all, black hair and eyes are much more beautiful than these pale colors, but this little one was so friendly. Something loving and

39

kind spread out from her like a light or a perfume. He tried to put her out of his mind, how she had trusted him, how she had spoken to him, how she had held out her two small hands, how she had cleaned his house, his cooking place, and his kettle.

He looked around for the bunch of flowers she had brought, and found them on one of the low benches. He filled half a coconut shell with water and put the flowers in it. Then he set the coconut-shell dish in the back window and was glad to see the twigs brighten and freshen during the day.

Tama knew that he must make important plans. It was not enough to call the Islam teachers. It was not enough to mark off a rich piece of garden land for them or even to build a house where they might live. No, he must think of some way to show the village people that the magic wand of the big teacher could be broken, that the teacher himself could be made to suffer because he taught things contrary to the spirits and had angered the devils that controlled the fire mountain.

He sorted over his charms and selected the three most powerful ones, a goat's skull, a huge shark's tooth, and a dried snake, which he had gotten from a mighty witch doctor on the big southern island. There were no such snakes on Sangir. Tama knew that everyone in the village respected his charms for the wonderful things they had done in times past. It was for him to choose now what kind of curse he would lay on them.

In the secret place of his lonely hut Tama called on all the devils of his acquaintance. He brought out the magic oil, mixed it with strong herbs, and smeared it all over his body. He rubbed it on the three charms, laying a powerful curse on each. Now he must arrange some plan so the big teacher would touch one of the charms. Then the evil magic was sure to work and there would be sickness or accident or some terrible calamity. The evil spirits sometimes made some surprising trouble that even the witch doctor couldn't foresee, but it always worked in the direction of punishing the one for whom the curse was laid.

Tama had just put all his charms away when Chief Meradin appeared. Tama invited him in.

"It is all arranged," the chief said. "I will take ten of the village men. I have chosen those who like to run to the teacher's house all the time. We are almost ready to leave now."

Tama laughed. "I have not been idle, you know. I have already prepared the devil charms. Now I must think of some way to put one of them in the teacher's way so he will have to touch it. Then...well, you know, anything might happen, but it will not be good for the teacher."

Chief Meradin laughed too. Both men felt in as merry a mood as Tama could remember.

"It seems to me that the fire mountain is quieter today," Chief Meradin said as he went down the ladder.

"Oh, those fire spirits will settle down as soon as we have taken care of this matter," Tama said.

Chief Meradin hesitated on the stairlike ladder. "There is another thing," he said. "I would like to take my son Satoo along with me, but if I do, you will have no chance to instruct him before the Islam teachers come. Also, if some bad thing happens to me ... well, you know it would be a great misfortune if both of us should be lost. You know our custom about chiefs."

"No, you should not take the boy. I can see that he has already been snared by the magic of these people, but I will break the magic. By the time you return I hope he will be as ready as you are to follow Islam."

Still the chief hesitated on the ladder. "It is my wish that you should use kindness and patient reasoning to bring this boy back to his senses. He will not respond to anger and force."

After the chief had gone, Tama decided that the best way to deal with Satoo was to tell him the truth and use persuasion to separate him from the teacher and the boy Hans.

Within an hour Tama saw a fishing boat pull away from the landing. He knew that the eleven men on board were not going after fish. They had sailed for the southern islands and when they returned they would bring the Mohammedan religion to Great Sangir.

Chapter Five

LEARNING ABOUT GOD

From the day the boy Hans came to the island of Sangir with his father, the big teacher, Satoo had been his friend. He had gone with him into the jungle to find rattan for binding the timbers of the building. He had helped carry rocks for the flower garden around the teacher's house. But it was not until the house and the fence and everything about the teacher's home and garden were finished, and Hans already knew many words of the island language, that Satoo led him one afternoon to his secret perch among the rocks where he loved to sit and watch the fire mountain.

The volcano looked closer from here. As the two boys climbed up among the rocks Satoo watched Hans's face and saw his blue eyes widen with surprise as he saw the huge form of the volcano so close. Smoke billowed from the cone-shaped top and spurts of fire shot into the sky. Here it was quiet, so quiet that the only sound was the lap of the waves on the shore below and the low rumble of thunder that came from deep under the sea floor.

Hans pointed down. "Why?"

"It is the fire spirits under the ground," Satoo explained. "They are angry, and when they are uncomfortable or displeased they always growl and thunder."

Hans shook his head. Satoo could see that he did not understand. He pointed to the volcano. "How far away do you think it is?"

Now Satoo understood the question his friend had asked, but he didn't know how to explain that the island people measure all distances by the time it takes them to travel to the place. He knew that men could row out to the volcano and back in the space of time between break fast and the middle of the day when the sun stands at mid-heaven. Satoo knew that sometimes the island men went out to get birds' eggs from the small sandy beach on the south side of the fire mountain. It was a brave thing to do, because everyone feared the fire spirits that lived there. But of course the eggs were delicious and worth risking something for.

"It is not far," Satoo said at last. "Can't you smell the smoke?"

Then Satoo explained how the island people in ancient times had offered human sacrifices to the mountain to quiet the fire spirits when they became unusually fierce and angry. Satoo could not remember, and his father could not remember, of the mountain smoking quite so much as now.

As the boys stood looking at the south side of the volcano Satoo saw something on the narrow beach of white sand that lay in a curve of the fire mountain's base.

Look!" He grabbed Hans's arm. "It's a big bird—a sea bird. That's the kind of bird that laid the eggs our men used to go after."

Hans shaded his eyes with his hand and looked. "It's so small, like an ant. I can hardly see it—Yes, I guess there is something there. It moves."

The boys watched the bird until it flew off toward the jungle north of them. Then they settled down in the perch among the rocks.

"Our witch doctor has come back," Satoo told Hans. "You know, the one who owns the hut where you lived at first. He came back last night. He says the fire spirits are angry because you came, but I think they are angry because my father wouldn't give the teacher a place to build his house."

This speech was too long for Hans to follow. Satoo laughed at him and said the words over and over until at last he saw that Hans did understand most of what he had said.

"Is the witch doctor there in the house where we lived?" Hans asked. "Is he there right now?"

"Yes, of course." Satoo laughed again. "Of course he is there. Where else would he be? It's his hut."

"My sister, little Marta, goes there every day to play house," Hans said. "I must go home and tell her not to go there any more. She might bother him. He will not like to have her come."

"Oh, he wouldn't hurt Marta. He is really a kind person. He is good to sick people and he even takes care of sick animals. He wouldn't hurt a little child."

"Of course no one would want to hurt Marta. I wasn't thinking of that," Hans said. "I just thought it might worry him."

The boys still gazed out over the calm sea and the smoking mountain, when the sound of oars disturbed them. They looked down at the little wharf and saw the village's largest fishing boat pulling away with several island men at the paddles.

Satoo stood up and strained his eyes to see better. Yes, it was his father's boat. Now, why hadn't they told him they were going fishing tonight? Why hadn't they taken him along?

"I don't like that," he said to Hans. "When my father's big boat goes out to catch fish, I always go."

Satoo saw the men put up the sail and tack toward the south. He could see them better now.

"You know, Hans," he said, "those men are all dressed in their feast clothes. They can't be going out to fish with

45

all their ornaments on and fixed up like that. They must be going to a feast somewhere on one of the southern islands."

Hans watched the boat. "Is that your father, there in the front of the boat?"

"You mean the one with his head turned away? No, I'm sure it isn't. He wouldn't go without me."

The two boys walked back to the house on the sand.

"Come on in the house and let us learn our verse for today," Hans said as they came to the low wall.

Inside, the teacher took down one of the magic boxes and opened it. Then he taught the boys their memory verse, "The Father, himself, loveth you."

Over and over the boys said the words until the teacher said they might go now to the jungle to get some thin pieces of rattan, because he needed to tie up the flower plants that were grown so big and bushy that some of them sagged and bent.

"What does the verse mean?" Satoo asked Hans as they walked across the salt grass toward the trees.

"The Father who loves us is God up in heaven." Hans pointed at the bright sun and the sky. "He lives up there among the stars and all the bright things, but He sees us all the time. He hears what we say. He is the one who loves us."

"Is it to this One that your father sings in the mornings and evenings?"

"Yes, my father sings because God makes his heart glad and I guess God likes to hear singing. All people who worship God sing."

"I have seen your father, the big teacher, talk to the magic boxes. I have heard him talk to the sky and the top of your house. Why does he do that?"

Hans smiled. "At worship time my father reads from the Holy Book; then we all kneel down and we lift up our eyes and pray to God. That means we talk to Him."

"You mean that you can talk to the God of heaven and He hears what you say?"

"Yes, of course. He talks to us in the verses like we learned today and in songs. We talk to Him when we pray."

By this time the boys had entered the jungle, and they slashed their way among the thick brush under the huge old trees looking for strands of the rattan vine. Most of what they found was too big and thick. After long searching they discovered a few small thin strings of young growth. This they wound up on their hands, being careful of the stickers. The vines were many feet in length and had already climbed to the tops of tall trees. The boys pulled and twisted to bring them down.

"If your father splits this, it should be just right for tying up the flowers," Satoo said as they started back.

Satoo walked first down the narrow trail they had cut. Hans was bigger than Satoo. He seemed to grow faster and he was stronger, but Satoo was quicker and he knew the jungle.

Today Satoo was eager to get home. He couldn't get that boat out of his thoughts. Where was the fishing boat going and why were so many village men in it and why were they all dressed up in their ornaments?

The boys heard a sound, a low cry. It could be a baby sobbing. They stopped on the trail and listened.

"It's a monkey," Satoo said. "It cries as though it may be hurt."

After a short search they found the tiny creature. He sat on the limb of a tree all alone. With every breath he cried and twisted. Even when Satoo climbed up to get

47

him he did not move. He wound his little arms around Satoo's wrist as the boy slid down through the tangle of vines and branches.

The boys turned him over and looked through his black fur, but there was no mark on him or any injury that they could find. He looked fat and healthy, but he cried until Satoo tied him in one corner of his loincloth.

"I will take him to Tama," the boy said. "He will know what ails him."

The two friends parted at the edge of the jungle. Hans took all the rattan in his hands, swinging the coils over his shoulders. Satoo took the tiny monkey and went toward Tama's house.

"I will see you when we sing this evening," he called back as he ran up the path.

Tama's door was open, and Satoo called in front of it the customary words of greeting. Tama came to the door and looked down at him. "Ah, I see you have brought me a sick monkey."

"How do you know he's sick?" Satoo asked as he ran up the ladder into the room.

"He must be sick or you could never have caught him. He would have followed his family into the treetops."

"You will make him better, won't you?" Satoo put the frightened little creature in Tama's hands.

"I will try," he said.

Tama brought out a little packet of herbs all dried and pounded fine. He mixed some of the green powder with water in a coconut-shell bowl and held it under the monkey's nose. The little fellow began to eat the mixture with greedy haste.

"You see," Tama said, "he knows what medicine is good for him. He must have eaten something that was

48

bad for him." Tama looked sharply at Satoo. "Boys do the same thing sometimes."

Satoo wondered whether the witchman thought that he had eaten some bad thing. He waited for Tama to say more, but the witchman stroked and petted the monkey, and after the tiny animal had snuggled down in Tama's loincloth and appeared to be asleep, Satoo asked, "Where did the fishing boat go just a little while ago?"

"It went to the southern islands," Tama said. "Your father, the chief, ordered it."

"But why? What is the reason? Our boats do not go on such long journeys for nothing. What does my father want them to bring from the southern islands?"

Tama's face grew stern. "Your father, the chief, intends to invite teachers of Islam to come here and lead our people in the good way."

Satoo felt his heart sink away toward some bottomless place. "Why does he do that? Already a teacher has come to our village and my father will not give him even enough ground to build a house. Why does he want more teachers?"

"The teachers of Islam are different," Tama explained. "They will not spoil our customs. They will not forbid our feasts and our dancing and our spirit worship. Of course we will have to get rid of our pigs. They don't like pigs. But we don't have many. We can make a big feast and eat them all up at once. They will expect us to do as we please. Don't you see? They will not change our ways as the big teacher is doing."

"If the Islam teachers will not change anything, then what is the use of having them?"

Tama's face softened a little and his voice was kind. "Now, Satoo, what is it you like so much about this big teacher's magic?"

"I like it that the God of heaven knows me and that I can talk to Him and He will talk with me. I like to feel the gladness running through me like a river when I hear the singing."

Then Tama laughed. "Foolish boy, not even the smallest spirits of the jungle will speak to a young boy like you. How then will a Great Spirit such as this God you talk about? What attention would He pay you?"

Satoo did not answer this question. He stood close to Tama and stroked the soft fur of the little monkey that lay curled in the witchman's loincloth.

"What will the teacher do when the Islam teachers come?" the boy asked.

"He will go away, of course, when he sees that the people would rather follow Islam."

Satoo looked straight into Tama's eyes. "He will not go away. You wait and see. And not all the people will choose Islam."

Tama smiled again, and Satoo choked down a cry of rage and ran from the room. He burst into his own door calling for his father in a loud voice, but Chief Meradin was not home.

"Where is my father, the chief?" he asked his mother, who tended the baby on her back and cooked at the same time.

"He has gone on a long journey, my son. He will not return for many days."

Then Satoo knew that the man he had seen in the front of the fishing boat was his father. Chief Meradin had gone himself to call Islam teachers to Great Sangir.

Chapter Six

THE SNAKE CHARM

Tama stood in the door of his hut and his eyes followed Satoo as the boy raced across the few rods between the two houses. The words Satoo had just spoken stood up in his mind like black stumps in a burned-over clearing. "He will not leave.... He will not leave."

Tama shook his head. The thing that shocked him was Satoo's fierce determination. He wondered whether all the village people who had listened to the big teacher's magic were so strong for the new teaching. For the first time he wondered whether it had been a wise thing to send for the new teachers of Islam. Up to this moment failure had not entered his mind. Now he was not sure. If the big teacher chose to stay and if a number of the village people wanted him to stay, and if they were all as stubborn as the chief's son, then there would surely be trouble.

Well, it was too late now. The messengers, with Chief Meradin, had already gone south to invite the Islam teachers. Tama felt certain they would come.

He took the monkey out and held it in his hands. He could see that the little animal felt better. He took a braided thong from the wall and fastened a wide bark belt around the monkey's middle, then tethered him just outside the door.

Tama made a fire in the clean clay stove, and as he worked he kept seeing a pair of little white hands brushing and cleaning the ashes from among the stones. He tried to shut thoughts of the little girl from his mind, because he needed to make plans. Now that he had put the heavy curses on his charms he must think of some plan to get them in the big teacher's way, so he would touch one of them.

51

Tama choked with horror as he saw Marta pick up the dried snake charm and stroke it gently while she crooned soft words of pity for it.

Also, while the chief was away he must prepare the people to receive the Islam teachers. He must find some way to prevent the villagers from flocking to the house on the sand, and he must do something to win Satoo away from his fanatical devotion to the teacher's family and the new magic they had brought.

With his mind still wandering, Tama prepared the cassava for his evening meal. He took it to the spring, and as he washed the roots he thought of the little girl with yellow braids and a pink dress who had scoured the kettle that morning. He tried to push thoughts of the child from his mind, but the first thing he saw when he climbed the ladder to his hut was the coconut shell in the window with the freshened sprigs of flowering twigs

Tama shook with sudden anger. Was this some kind of witchcraft? He set the kettle over the stones, rushed to the window, and flung both shell and blossoms out to ward the jungle. Then he kindled his fire.

While he waited for the kettle to boil he unwrapped his charms. He handled them with care, for the curses he had laid on the principal charms were so powerful that he feared them himself. He laid the goat's skull, the shark's tooth, and the dried snake by themselves on a piece of bark cloth and put the others away. Before he sat down to eat he looked out at the fire mountain. The ground had quivered several times during the day. Smoke and flame belched from the volcano's mouth almost all the time and the rumblings under the ground sounded worse than usual.

He dished up his meal and sat down to eat, and as he ate he planned what he would do. First, he intended to scare the village people about the fire spirits. They feared the mountain, and certainly he could make them see that it was because of the new teacher that the volcano spit smoke and flame. The fire spirits must be furi-

53

ous. He didn't think he would have much trouble convincing them of that. Then he would let them know that he would use his most deadly charms against the teacher. When the bad things began to happen he would soon have the village people back under his control again.

It was evening when Tama finished his food. He had been home for almost a day already, and not one person had come to call him. The chief had come on the first night and Satoo came this afternoon, but they had not come for medicine. Then, of course, the little child came. But what could have happened to the village folks? Usually some sick or troubled person called him several times a day, and after he had been away for so long, there must be sick persons and worried ones that needed his help.

Tama remembered that the last time he came back from a journey to the other side of the island there had been people waiting outside his hut from the moment they knew he was home.

The witch doctor looked out his door again. He saw village men and women walking down toward the teacher's house. Anger shook him again. This, then, was the reason no one came to ask for medicine or to call him to help the sick or to tell him their troubles and ask for advice.

Just look at them! There must be at least ten people going down the path right now. That big teacher had stolen their hearts. They had taken their evening baths at the spring and eaten their evening meal. They ought to be inside their houses getting ready to sleep. Instead, here they were flocking down the path to the teacher's house. And what did they intend to do there?

Tama remembered his visit to the teacher's house the night before, just a little later than this. He remembered the singing and how it had struck him down with its beauty and power and how he had lain shocked and confused in the salt grass outside the low rock wall.

The village people must be going over to hear that singing. He supposed they went every night to listen to it. There was probably no way to stop them tonight. It might be a good thing to follow them and see what would happen in the big teacher's house.

As he swung down the ladder and along the path the witchman saw more people come out of their houses. They hurried toward the teacher's house, as though they were afraid they might miss something.

He overtook one of the young men from the village with a baby in his arms.

"Where do you go?" Tama asked.

"Oh, don't you know? We go every night to hear the singing and the magic from the black boxes."

Tama didn't say anything. The young man turned and looked at him. "Oh, you don't need to worry about his magic. It is all good. This baby of mine was sick yesterday, and the big teacher came and gave him medicine. He said the magic words to his God, and he sat with us until the child was better. Now, you see, the baby is well again."

Now Tama knew for certain why the village people had not come to take his medicine or ask help. Anger rose again in his stomach, but he put it down and questioned the young man about the teacher and his family until they stood before the gate into the teacher's garden. Tama had not meant to go inside the house, but now he could not avoid going in. The villagers swept him along with them, but he was a little curious too.

In the front room of the house clean mats were spread, and the room was already almost filled with eager people. The teacher sat in a corner of the room.

Tama stared at him. Even as he sat there on a mat cross-legged, Tama could see that he was the biggest man who had ever lived on this island. The hair of his head and beard was red and curly—a red-haired giant, that's what he was. The big man laughed and talked to the village people as they came in. He called them by name. He called the children by name. He held a block of magic in his hands. Tama's anger came back. The mats were crowded with people. No one moved over to make room for him. He decided to go home.

Then he felt a small hand tug at his, and looked down into the face of the little girl who had visited his hut this morning. She smiled up at him and whispered something in her own language. She pulled on his hand. Tama allowed her to lead him into another room of the house. He understood that this little one was proud of the new house, that she knew he had never been inside before and wanted to show it to him.

The witchman saw that everything in the house was as neat as the garden outside. The teacher's wife had arranged the four rooms of the house so that one was used for cooking and eating, two for sleeping, and the largest one for visitors.

Tama looked at the high platforms these people used for sleeping. Each one was covered with something that should have been a mat but wasn't. These covers were made of so many bright colors that they bewildered Tama's eyes. He laid his hand on one of the platforms. The cover felt soft and he stroked it. The child led him back into the big room and found him a comfortable sitting place where he could lean back against the wall. Then she sat down beside him. She had not let go of his hand.

Tama fumbled around for his anger, but it was gone. The child's hand was still warm in his. Clearly she had chosen him for a friend. The witch doctor was not accustomed to the feel of a child's hand. There was something reassuring about it.

The teacher spoke now in the language of the island. True, his speech stumbled and halted and was filled with mistakes, but the man's voice was friendly and the meaning of what he said was clear. Tama could see that the big teacher loved the people who sat here before him, and in spite of his imperfect talk he was able to make them understand the kindness he offered them.

When the man opened the block of magic and began speaking to it, his deep rich voice took on a solemn tone that awed the people. The room quieted; even the children hushed their giggles and their whimpering. The magic pressed Tama with its power, but he resisted it. He looked down at the little girl beside him. She had laid her head on his knee, and one of her yellow braids fell across his hand. The silky hair lay soft and warm against it. The little one is sleepy, Tama thought, and smiled in spite of himself.

Then the teacher closed the magic box and began to sing. The small girl sprang up, pulled her hand away from Tama's, and went to stand beside her father. As the rich melody flowed through the room she sang along with her father, every note as perfect as his, but in a higher tone. The teacher's wife sang well, too, and so did the boy. Some of the village people tried to make the beautiful sounds, but they hadn't learned very well yet. Tama saw several of them look at him as though they felt embarrassed or timid in his presence.

Again Tama felt the power of the singing as he had felt it the night before. Terrible fear overwhelmed him. He leaped to his feet and rushed out into the dark. He ran all the way up to the village.

All out of breath the witchman scrambled up the little ladder of his hut. Then he flung himself down in the doorway and gazed out into the night. He could still hear the singing in the teacher's house. It came faintly through the air, and even from this distance it shook him with fear. He glanced at the glowing cone of the fire mountain in the curve of the bay. Even as Tama sat there recovering his breath the earth quivered. Yes, the fire spirits were very angry, and they had good reason to be angry. Then the song ended. Tama relaxed.

"Ah, you are here, Tama?" A voice spoke out of the darkness. "I see you do not go to drink the new magic and the music."

Tama peered into the night and made out the form of old Gola, the chief's eldest adviser and counselor.

"Are we the only ones in the village who do not run after the new magic?" Tama asked.

"I think the others are all over there." The old man hobbled up the ladder and into the room. "I think most of them go only out of curiosity. They will run after any new thing. You know that."

"It is not good, Gola. It is dangerous. Look at that fire mountain. Do you think the spirits are happy about this new teaching that has come to Great Sangir?"

"No, of course not, but we must be patient. The chief will certainly bring the Islam teachers., They will also be new. They will have magic too and they will have wonderful things to do and say. They will make their kind of witchcraft and the people will run after that too."

"Do you think so?" Tama pulled a mat up to the door and they both sat down close together. "You see, Gola, some of these people have already been taken in the heart...that is bad."

"Yes, it is too bad about the chief's son. How can he ever be chief if he follows this strange magic? What will his father do? He has no other son. Chief Meradin should have called you back sooner."

"Satoo has made his heart strong for the new teaching," Tama said. "We must think of some way to break the power of the magic for him. Ordinary advice will not move him."

"Perhaps it is not yet too late." Gola's voice sounded courageous. "You have powerful charms, you know."

"Yes." Tama's voice vibrated with excitement. "I have already laid the curse. Tomorrow I will call the spirits again and plant the devil magic."

"Good, good." Gola chuckled and stood up to leave. Long after the old man had gone Tama lay on his sleeping mat and thoughts tumbled through his mind. Of course he had the charms. Either the teacher's family would sicken, perhaps die, or there might be a bad accident. Some terrible thing was sure to happen. His charms had always worked on the island people. There could be no reason why they wouldn't work on these foreign teachers.

Then other thoughts pushed into his mind. The picture of the little girl with the yellow braids came up. He saw her stricken with fever, shaken with chills, thin with the starving sickness—all these he was able to bring on the teacher's family. These thoughts made him squirm and twist on his mat, and a dreadful fear struck him. Had the teacher's magic already taken hold of him?

Tama did not sleep that night. When he heard the monkey cry he got up and turned the little creature loose and watched while it swung up into the trees in the edge of the jungle.

Morning climbed the sky over the fire mountain, and he was ashamed and angry. With a vicious swing he picked up the black kettle and went down to the spring to prepare his breakfast. The spring was behind the house and a short distance into the jungle, but the path was a well-beaten trail, for most of the village men used that spring for bathing.

Tama lingered a long time at the spring. He bathed; he shook himself. He drew in deep breaths of the cool moist air. At last he felt better. He knew he could face what he must do this day. He filled the black kettle with enough water to cook the taro he had washed and went back to his hut.

The door stood open as he had left it. His three most powerful charms still lay on the floor where he had put them yesterday, but now a little girl with yellow braids and a pink dress sat beside them. A scream of horror choked in Tama's throat as she picked up the dried snake and stroked it gently while she crooned soft words as though she pitied the poor dead creature.

Tama dropped the kettle of water, and with a great splash it clattered on the ladder and thumped to the ground.

Chapter Seven

TAMA'S VICTORY

Satoo had seen little Marta climb the ladder to the witchman's hut. He stood for a moment thinking about what he must do. After the words he had spoken to Tama last night it was not good for him to go and take the child away. He must run to the house on the beach and tell Hans. Hans would know what to do.

"Hans, Hans!" Satoo stood all out of breath at the teacher's door and called, "Hans, come."

Hans came out, his shock of red hair glittering in the bright sunshine and his jolly face laughing.

"Hans, Marta has gone to the witchman's house. I think you should go and bring her out. Tama may want to make medicine today, and he will not like to be disturbed."

"Yes, yes, let's go." Hans loped off up the beach and into the path that led to the village. Satoo followed. Within five minutes the two boys stood at the foot of the ladder that led tip into Tama's house.

"Look, this is Tama's cooking pot!" Satoo pointed to the black pot upside down at the foot of the ladder. "Now, why do you suppose he threw it down there?"

Then a strange sound came from the hut. Both boys shook with fear. It was the sound of something that groaned and gasped in agony and terrible pain. Satoo's spine prickled and the hairs along the back of his neck stung like poison seaweed. It took all his courage to climb the ladder far enough to look in through the open door.

Tama stood in the middle of the hut holding Marta in his arms. His face was hidden against her bright hair and the awful sounds were coming from him.

"Marta!" Hans called to her in a quivering voice.

She scrambled out of the witchman's arms and ran to the boys. Tama fell forward on the floor, with his face pressed to the split bamboo, and the groans and sobs that twisted his body were like those of a wounded animal. Even after they led Marta away, Satoo could still hear the heartbreaking sound, and the terror inside his own stomach could not be quieted.

"Hans," he said, after they had put Marta safely inside the stone fence. "Hans, I think Tama is making powerful medicine. I never saw him make that kind before. Ask Marta what she did in Tama's house."

Both boys talked to Marta, but the only word they could get from her was that she had "blessed the poor snake."

Satoo puzzled over this for a long time before he understood. "I think I know. She must have gotten hold of one of Tama's devil charms—a dried snake."

"Is that why Tama lay on the floor and moaned like that?"

"I don't know." A terrible thought had come to Satoo's mind. "I think there is a bad curse on anyone who touches a devil charm. Oh, Hans, something terrible will come to Marta now! Hurry, run and tell your father, so he can make the strong medicine of God."

Hans laughed. "Oh, Satoo, devil medicine and snake charms can't hurt us. You see, witchcraft has no power against those who worship God."

Satoo was not convinced. He still stood trying to put away the fear that had dropped over him like a heavy cloud. "For us...oh, Hans, for us it is horrible. I cannot help fearing for Marta."

"Well, come, let's talk to my father." Hans drew his friend into the room where the big teacher sat among his boxes of magic.

After Hans had explained in the strange language of these people, the teacher turned to Satoo. "Don't be afraid." He spoke slowly in the island tongue. "The God we worship does not allow us to be hurt by devil charms. Let us kneel right here and tell Him what has happened. Then you will feel better."

So the three of them knelt in the quiet room, and although Satoo could not understand the words that the big teacher spoke to his God, they soothed away the terror from his mind and for the first time he felt God's comforting presence.

Later as the boys roamed along the beach, Satoo asked so many questions about God and His magic that Hans could not follow his talk. "You want to know so many things so fast," he said.

"Did the teacher tell God all about Tama?" he asked for the third time. "I mean, did he tell God that Tama is lying there on his floor moaning and groaning?"

"Yes, he told God the whole thing," Hans said. "He asked God to catch Tama just like a man catches his little child who tries to run away from him into danger.

Satoo tried to picture it in his mind, a great big man, much bigger than the big teacher, running along the jungle path after Tama.

He smiled. "You think God will catch him?"

"My father says God already has his hand on Tama, but he is still kicking and fighting and trying to get away.

The boys climbed up to Satoo's secret lookout perch among the rocks. Here the fire mountain loomed before them. Today it vomited out flame, and the boys could hear the sea hiss as fiery molten stone hit the water.

Satoo strained his eyes, searching the narrow strip of white sand. No birds today. The noise and fire of the mountain had driven the birds away." Those fire spirits are surely angry," Satoo said to Hans. "I have never seen them so angry."

He wanted to tell Hans about the powerful medicine Tama could make and how everyone on Great Sangir feared his curses more than they feared the fire mountain. He wanted to tell Hans that the men of Sangir, along with his own father, had gone to the southern islands to bring Islam teachers. There was so much to tell and the words they both understood, so few. It was like trying to push a river through a hollow straw.

"Hans." He decided to try anyhow. "My father has gone to bring Islam teachers."

"What are they?"

"They are teachers, maybe like your father. They will teach the magic of Islam."

"So that's where the boat went yesterday." Hans grinned. Satoo could see that he was not troubled by this news.

"You see"—Satoo spoke slowly and tried to make every word clear—"Tama is behind this. He wants to drive your father away from this island."

Now Hans laughed. "Of course Tama can't drive my father away by his witch charms. God told my father to come here, so of course nobody can drive him away."

"But the Islam teachers may keep the people from coining to hear the words from God's Holy Book. That wouldn't be good."

"No, that wouldn't be good." Hans agreed. "But God is strong. He can take care of that all right."

And on that day, among the coral rocks of their secret perch, Hans taught Satoo to pray and to talk to God reverently, but as to a friend.

Comforted by their prayers and their talk, the boys sat for a long time and watched the fire spout from the volcano. The sun had risen to midheaven and the rocks burned their feet. They ran down to the beach and waded in the cool water and hunted for crabs and shells until Hans's mother called him to come to eat.

Then Satoo wandered back toward the village. He glanced over toward the witchman's house and saw that the black pot still lay upside down at the foot of the little ladder.

Again a terrible fear struck the island boy. It was now past midday. Tama had not eaten his morning meal yet. He had not even come out of his house. Maybe the witchman was sick, or maybe…Satoo's spine tingled with pure horror…maybe Tama was making the most powerful spirit medicine that had ever been made on this island.

Satoo thought about what Hans had told him of how God was running after Tama and trying to catch him, and Satoo thought that Tama was way out where even God couldn't get hold of him this time. Hans just didn't know. The big teacher didn't know. They hadn't seen how Tama's witch medicine worked.

Satoo talked to his mother about what he had seen in Tama's house, but she told him not to worry. Tama was a strong man and not very old either, that he knew how to mind his own business, and would appreciate it if everyone else minded theirs.

Still, Satoo could not forget the agonized groans he had heard that morning, and he couldn't help worrying about Marta. After he had eaten he went past Tama's house again.

The kettle was gone. The boy sighed with relief. At least Tama was still alive. And what was he planning against the big teacher? Satoo shuddered. It must be something dreadful.

Three days passed, and Satoo watched Tama's hut, because he could see it plainly from his own house, or at a greater distance from the beach and the teacher's house. While his father was away Satoo spent all his time in one of these three places, and he kept his eyes on the witchman's hut so constantly that he was sure Tama could not leave or enter the hut without his knowing it. So far as Satoo could discover, the witchman neither bathed nor cooked food.

On the fourth evening Satoo went to the jungle spring to bathe. He always came to this spring now, curious to know what the witch doctor might be doing.

Tama came down to the spring, and Satoo was startled at the look of his face. It was drawn and pale. He drooped with sadness and misery.

"Do you still go all the time to the teacher's house?" Tama asked him.

"Yes, I go every day, because Hans is my friend."

"Are they all well?" Tama stooped under the stream of water and began to wash himself.

"They are all well. Why shouldn't they be?" Satoo stood still and waited for the witchman to answer, but he said nothing more. He bathed, filled his kettle, and went back to his hut with the same sad, closed face, and Satoo stared after him.

"Now what can be making him so miserable?" Satoo asked himself. "Is he grieved because the teacher's family are not sick?"

Satoo could see that few of the village people went to take medicine from Tama, and he did not go to any of the village houses, but the old counselman, Gola, was busy every day. He went from hut to hut and spent all his time talking. Satoo knew what he told the people. He told them that great new magic was about to come to the island. Chief Meradin had discovered that his people were fond of new magic, so he had gone to bring them the finest magic of all, and they should get ready to welcome the new teachers.

When the villagers asked what would become of the big teacher and his magic when the new teachers came, Gola told them that they could choose between the two kinds of magic, but he was sure they would all choose to follow Islam, because they would not need to leave off any of their old customs.

Gola persuaded several of the village men to mark off a big piece of garden land right above the teacher's house on the sand, but higher up the slope of a fertile hill. Satoo watched them do it. They drove sticks into the ground and even wove a low fence of reeds, and Gola began to clear the spot. He dragged away brush and fallen branches and trimmed the fruit trees that stood inside the marked-off area.

"Now why didn't Chief Meradin let the big teacher have this ground?" one of the village men remarked as he helped with the work. "This would have been a fine place for him to make a beautiful garden here."

"The big teacher is not going to stay here," Gola said, "so of course he doesn't need any place."

So the talk was closed for the moment, but Satoo heard it whispered on all sides that the chief had made a big mistake in forcing the teacher to make his home on the sand. By rights he should have had this fine plot of ground that was being readied for the Islam teachers.

If Gola heard the talk, he gave no sign and paid no attention. He went every day to clear and trim and make the place nice for the strangers, who would be coming any day now. Tama did not go near the place. Satoo saw him every day, and each day he looked more sick and miserable than he had the day before.

Then Satoo found out that Tama went at night to watch beside the teacher's house. It was by accident that Satoo discovered this. He had gone to bed when he remembered that he had left his best knife stuck in the trough where the teacher's flowers grew. He crept out of his hut and streaked along the path down to the beach. He was not afraid, because he knew that no bad spirits lived near the teacher's house, and it was not a good thing to leave the knife in the wet soil of the flower trough overnight.

He had just drawn out the knife and turned back from the darkened house when he saw something move. It was a bent figure standing close to the children's window. With a surge of desperate fear, Satoo fled along the path back to his hut.

He looked back twice, but although the moon gave enough light to see things distinctly, he was sure no person followed him. Then he wondered whether he had imagined the dark form crouched. there at the children's window.

He sat just inside the door of his own hut and waited.

He waited for a long time, and then he saw a figure coming slowly along the path. Even before the person turned aside to climb the ladder of his hut, Satoo knew it was Tama.

When Satoo went to retrieve his knife stuck in the flower trough he found out that Tama went at night to watch the teacher's house.

The boy felt his heart quicken in his naked chest. What could this mean? Why should Tama be watching the teacher's house? And why at the children's window? Had he been going there every night? Why? Why?

It was late when Satoo finally got to sleep, and his mother had to waken him the next morning. He went down to the spring and bathed and sat eating his fish and taro when he heard a voice calling outside his door. He jumped up to welcome his friend Hans. He looked into Hans's usually jolly face, but this morning it was troubled.

"Satoo, is Marta here?"

"Why no," Satoo said. "I just woke up a few minutes ago. I haven't seen her." Satoo felt something black and heavy fasten itself upon him.

"Come with me," Hans said. "Perhaps she has gone to the witchman's house. My father told her not to go there, but maybe she forgot."

The boys ran over to Tama's door and called loudly in front of it, but there was no answer. The door stood open, and the boys climbed the ladder and looked in. There was nothing to see. The hut was in order, but Tama was not there, and there was no trace of Marta.

"We don't know how long she has been gone," Hans said. "She ate her breakfast and went outside to play as she always does."

"She must be somewhere around the village." Satoo tried to comfort his friend. "Maybe she went up to our perch among the rocks. You remember she tried to follow us up there a couple of times."

The boys raced for the beach and clambered up to the perch among the rocks, but no little girl was there, and without a glance at the smoking fire mountain they hurried down again.

The black weight dragged heavy on Satoo now. Should he tell Hans that he had seen Tama crouching outside the children's window last night? Could Tama possibly have anything to do with Marta's disappearance?

The boys saw the big teacher hurrying along the path. They ran after him and overtook him just as he entered the village. He called the people from every hut to ask if they had seen Marta and to urge them to come and help look for her.

At Gola's hut, when he stopped and called, both Tama and Gola came out. When Tama heard the teacher's words, his face twisted and his whole body shook. He almost fell down the ladder of Gola's hut, but he stumbled down and took hold of the big teacher's arm. He could not speak.

Chapter Eight

ISLAM'S VICTORY

Satoo stood beside his friend Hans, but fear paralyzed him and he could not take his eyes from the witch doctor, who clutched the big teacher's arm and moaned as though someone had struck him with a spear.

The teacher patted Tama's shoulder and tried to soothe him enough so he could talk. All the people had run out of their huts and stood watching and listening. They could all understand what the red-haired man was trying to say. He kept asking Tama, "Where is Marta? Do you know where Marta is?"

Tama shook his head. It seemed to Satoo that all Tama could do now was to shake his head over and over, but at last he spoke in a choked voice. "I didn't see her...I didn't see her...It is the curse—the snake curse."

The big teacher didn't understand at first. He still patted Tama's shoulder and tried to figure out what the witchman had said, but the man's voice was so strangled and full of quivers that even Satoo could scarcely make out the words. Finally Satoo went to the teacher. He stood right in front of him and told him what Tama had said. He sounded every word by itself, so the red-haired man could understand.

"He says he doesn't know where Marta is, but he thinks something bad has happened to her because of the snake curse."

A smile spread over the big teacher's face. "What is this snake curse he talks about?"

It must be some curse he has laid against your family," Satoo said. "He has powerful spirit charms, you know. He has teeth and skulls of animals and roots and seeds, but his strongest charm is a dried snake."

"Oh, that must be what Marta told us about when she went to Tama's house the other day," Hans said. "She said she 'blessed the poor snake,' remember?"

Satoo shivered. "She must have picked the snake up. Tama had already laid the curse on it, I suppose. This is dangerous, you know." He took hold of Hans and shook him a little. "Something bad has surely happened to Marta. Tama's curses always work."

Satoo looked at Tama. He thought he had never seen anyone's face so miserable. Everyone stood there looking at the witchman. The teacher looked at him too, but he still kept his hand on Tama's shoulder.

Look here, my friend," the big teacher said. "We don't know where Marta is, but I'm sure she is all right. She must have wandered off somewhere. Now all you people stand right here where you are. I will ask the God we worship to show you that the snake curse cannot touch those who worship Him."

Then the red-haired man lifted his eyes and talked to the sky. The words he said were loud and powerful, and the people trembled although they couldn't understand.

When the words were finished the big teacher smiled and said to Tama, "Now, help us; we must find the child. She cannot have gone far. She has only been gone since we ate breakfast this morning."

It was Tama who found Marta, and Satoo was right behind him. They had pushed into the jungle, past the spring, and there they found the little girl with a bunch of wildflowers in her hand. She had stripped them from a jungle vine. When Tama came toward her she held both arms out to him and tried to give him the bouquet of blossoms.

The witch doctor lifted her in his arms and held her close. Satoo walked behind them, and he saw the shaking of Tama's shoulders and knew that the witchman tried to put down his great joy at finding little Marta unhurt.

At the spring they met the whole village, for every one seemed to have the same idea—that Marta must have gone into the jungle. Tama put the child in her father's arms and turned to go back to his hut.

The teacher took hold of his arm. "Tama, you see the child is unhurt. You are not to grieve or worry any more. No spirit curses can hurt this little girl."

Satoo and Hans stood close to the big teacher. They watched Tama go back to his hut. "You see," the big man said, "he loves little Marta. He is afraid of his own witch medicine." He looked down at the two boys. "God is pulling on Tama's heart. You will see."

It was evening of the next day when someone saw the chief's fishing boat. It was still only a speck on the horizon, but excitement ran through the village like a flame, and all the people flocked to the landing place and waited for the boat to pull in to the wharf. Hans was there with Satoo, and both boys strained for the first view of the teachers of Islam.

There were three of them, smiling brown men with faces much like the people of Great Sangir. Two of them were young, but one—Satoo was sure he must be the leader—was older. He wore a red cap on his head and Satoo thought his eyes looked cold, like polished pebbles in the water.

All the men acted friendly to everyone, and when the chief led them to his own house, the whole village followed, and watched to see what the newcomers would do and say. For one thing, Satoo knew already that these men spoke the language of his people easily. He had heard their voices. He also heard the name of the short stocky man who was their leader. He was called Guru Mula.

The following morning Chief Meradin sent a messenger to every house in the village telling them that now he would make a great feast because the new teachers had come. It would be a feast of welcome, and the people must all cook and bring their best palm wine and make merry in order to show the new teachers honor and kindness, because these men had brought wonderful new magic from the southern islands. The feast was set for the fourth day from then.

Immediately the whole village seethed with excitement. In every house the women began preparation for the feast. Tama came out of his house and mingled with the village people and acted like his old self again.

Only in the house on the sand was there no change and no excitement. There was only the beautiful singing at morning and evening and a great deal of looking into the black Book and still more of talking to the God of heaven.

Satoo had learned at last that when the big teacher lifted his eyes to the sky or to the roof of the house he was talking to God, who lived far beyond all things that men can see, up, up behind the stars.

Another thing that Satoo had learned was that when the teacher opened the Holy Book and laid it on his knees, he was not talking to the Book of magic; he was reading from it words that had been written there long ago, so long ago that no living man could remember back so far.

The evening after the feast was announced, only a few people came to the house on the sand to hear the singing and the words of God. Satoo came and a few others, but the rest of the village people were so eager to prepare for the great feast that they had no time for singing or listening. They were so busy that most of them had no time or thought for the fire mountain.

The day after the Islam teachers came, Satoo went alone to his perch high among the rocks. He sat there for a long time trying to collect his thoughts and to understand what was happening around him in the village. One thing he knew for certain, the battle between the magic of the big teacher and the new teaching of Islam had already begun and that his father, Chief Meradin, was on the side of the Islam teachers.

As he sat there and wondered what might happen next, he could not help seeing that now the fire mountain seemed to throw out more fire than it ever had before, and the trembling of the ground was more than usual, and even the sound of the deep growlings and thunderings in the solid earth rumbled louder than Satoo remembered. If the fire spirits had been angry before, now they raged with fury.

The feast was to last three days, and most of those three days Satoo ran back and forth between the village and the house on the sand. In the village all was wild excitement. The people danced and chanted and fought and drank and gorged on the food the women had prepared.

In the teacher's house all was quiet except for the singing. The big teacher sang all the time these days, and Satoo couldn't understand why. Surely he must have seen what the chief had done. He couldn't help knowing about the fine piece of garden land the chief had given the new teachers. And Satoo was sure he felt sorry be cause the village people did not come as they used to, to listen and learn the words of the songs and the words from the Holy Book. Now they were busy feasting. Had they forgotten so soon? Yet, Satoo thought, the melodies had never sounded so sweet, and it was a pity, too, because there were so few to listen.

During the days of the feast the big teacher went out to fish, and Satoo could hear him singing even out on the water.

"Why does your father sing?" Satoo asked Hans on the last day of the feast. "There is no one to hear."

Hans looked at him in surprise. "My father doesn't sing to people. He sings to God."

"Why?" It was Satoo's turn to be astonished.

"Well, it's like this. He knows how good and great and strong God is and all the wonderful things God will do, so he sings to thank God for all these things."

"And do you think God listens?"

"Of course He listens. It makes Him glad to hear my father sing. Wait, you will see what God will do."

After the feast some of the people were sick. It was a common thing after feasts for people to become sick. Satoo didn't know why, but Hans said it might be because they ate too much or drank too much palm wine and maybe the food wasn't clean.

Satoo wondered about this. He had always thought that evil spirits make people sick, and he could never figure out why, just after a big feast, when the people had sacrificed to the spirits and praised and honored them, the ungrateful spirits should turn right around and make so many people sick. Perhaps Hans was right. Satoo began to wonder whether the evil spirits were as powerful as he had thought.

Whatever stomachaches the people of Sangir had, they did not trouble the big teacher with them. They flocked to Tama for his witch medicine.

During the next few weeks there was great activity on the hill back of the teacher's house, for the village men were putting up a fine house for the Islam teachers. They brought poles and timbers from the jungle and the women wove matting and thatch at the chief's command. They did not stop with building one house. They built three, and all of them were bigger and better than the teacher's house on the sand. But none of them were so neat and none of them had a garden of bright flowers hugging its walls. None of them had a little girl like Marta or a boy like Hans. So Satoo chose to go more and more to the teacher's house. It was harder for him to go now, because his father scolded him and threatened to punish him, but still he went.

The leader of the Islam teachers, Guru Mula, persuaded the chief to build a house for worship. Only the men could go to the worship house. No women were allowed. The whole thing was mysterious to Satoo, and there was no singing. He could not understand why his father should be so strong for this kind of magic.

However, just as Gola had said, there were many of the village people who listened to the new magic. Also there were some who came back to the teacher's house to worship after the first excitement had passed.

By the time the rainy season began, the village had divided into two parts. The greater part of the people followed the new teaching of Islam, and a smaller group—about thirty persons—chose to follow the big teacher. Among these was Satoo. Even though his father often slapped him and Guru Mula scolded and they urged him to attend the Islam worship, the boy steadfastly refused, and now the ties of faith and friendship drew him even closer to the teacher's family than before.

This was true of all the little flock of village people who worshipped in the house on the sand. It was as though a great hand enfolded them and squeezed them together until they were as one heart and one mind.

Now their minds opened to the teaching and they quickly learned the songs. Little by little they began to look different from the other people of the village. Their faces shone with a kind of brightness; their bodies were cleaner and stronger. Their huts were neater, and most different of all, they went about their work singing the songs the big teacher taught them. They understood now that God rejoiced to hear their songs, because when He listened to their sweet songs of praise, He knew that they trusted Him for everything.

"I suppose the Islam teachers are quite happy now," Hans said as he loitered with Satoo on the beach.

"Oh, I wouldn't say that," Satoo answered. "Gola is grinning all the time. Maybe he is happy. My father, the chief, is unhappy because the big teacher is not going to leave Great Sangir, and of course he is angry with the people who keep on worshipping here in your house. Tama is always sad. I never saw him so sour-faced."

"Do you remember what my father said about Tama the day Marta was lost?" Hans asked his friend. "Do you remember how he said that God is pulling on Tama's heart?"

"Why would that make Tama so miserable?"

"If something is pulling on you and you resist it and fight with it, you might not be happy either—you might even hurt."

"Yes, I suppose so," Satoo agreed. "Another thing, Tama promised the people that if they accepted the Islam teachers, the fire spirits would be comforted and they would lie down and rest and not make all that noise and fire and shaking."

Both boys looked at the volcano.

79

"It looks to me as if that fire mountain is spouting out more flame than ever," Hans said.

"Yes, no one has seen any birds over there since the Islam teachers came. Everyone is worried. Now they say that the only way to quiet the spirits is to chase your family away."

"Of course you know it isn't spirits that make the fire," Hans said. "There are volcanoes in other lands. My father says there are fires deep in the earth."

"My father has called a counsel for this evening, Satoo said. "And they will decide what to do. They are so worried about the fire mountain they will surely do something." Satoo laid his hand on Hans's arm. "Whatever I hear I will tell you. Don't worry. I know that God is strong and He will take care of us."

Chapter Nine

A WITCH DOCTOR'S STRUGGLE

The Islam teachers had been on Great Sangir for four months. Already their teaching had won most of the villagers to the Mohammedan religion, but things had not gone the way Tama the witchman planned. He had seen that the big red-haired teacher was kind to everyone, even those who did not follow the teaching of his God, or come to his house to sing and pray. He treated all the people with kindness and respect.

But this was not true of the Islam teachers, especially Guru Mula. No sooner had he brought most of the village folks under his influence than he began to persecute those who chose to worship at the big teacher's house on the sand.

Most important of those who followed the Christian teaching was Satoo, son of Chief Meradin. Everyone in the village knew that he would be the next chief, and they could not see how it would be possible for him to continue to worship God as the big teacher taught, and still become chief.

Now Tama sat with Chief Meradin, Guru Mula, and the other two Mohammedan teachers in the new house where Guru Mula lived by himself. Evening had come and the sun had already set over the ridge of hills that ran down the length of Great Sangir like the knobby humps on a big lizard's back. They did not talk much at first. They all watched the mountain. Even when black night came down it was not really dark, for the flaming cone of the volcano lighted the sky with a weird unearthly light that changed and fluttered with each breath of the fire mountain. As the night winds blew back and forth Tama could sometimes catch a whiff of the mountain's foul odor.

Never in all his life could Tama remember such wild and furious thunderings from the volcano, such spurts of red fire and shooting forth of glowing stones. Along with all the other village people he took comfort from the thought that the mountain was at least two miles out in the ocean. At least its stream of fire could not burn their village or harm any of them.

The chief had talked of moving the village away to some other part of the island, but none of the people wanted to move. Their gardens and homes were here, and after all, the fire mountain had always been there, even in their great-grandfathers' days. Stories of the volcano and the fire spirits had come down to them from as far back as their tribal legends reached into the past. The thing to do was to make strong medicine that would quiet the fire spirits.

"Did you call your son, Satoo, to come here to night?" Guru Mula finally asked the chief.

Yes, he will come. I see him coming now."

Satoo came up the ladder into the house, and with a polite greeting to the Islam teachers and Tama, he sat down beside his father. His eyes were clear and his skin fresh and healthy-looking. Satoo had grown fast in the last six months and now stood tall and strong, almost as tall as his father.

But the thing Tama noticed most about him was the change in his manner. The boy seemed bursting with some secret joy that shone out of him like the light from a coconut-oil lamp, but with it there was a tenderness, a gentle way of treating everyone, not with arrogance, as was often the custom of a young chief, but with respect.

Tama had watched the boy about his work in his father's garden or in the jungle. He had listened to his songs. Yes, he had learned to make the beautiful sounds like the big teacher. His voice had changed too. Perhaps it was from singing so much. It was deeper now, and there was kindness in it. Among all the children of the village Satoo was the brightest, the most handsome, the most promising. The witchman saw how Chief Meradin's eyes rested on his son with pride and great sadness.

The Guru spoke to Satoo. "We have called the young chief here this evening to talk about the worship of the village."

"I am a worshiper," Satoo said without hesitation. "I worship God and His Son Jesus. I worship according to the teachings of God's Holy Book."

Guru Mula waved his hand in an impatient gesture as though to brush away what Satoo had said. "Yes, we know that. It is for that reason we have brought you here. It is our wish that you should worship Allah according to the rules of the Mohammedan faith. It is not fitting that the chief's son should follow a handful of foolish persons who persist in running after the crazy things this red-haired foreigner tells them."

"Ah, no, I will never change." Satoo looked at the Islam leader with a smile on his handsome face. "I couldn't do that. I love my father and my mother and I belong to our island people, but no, I will never change."

"You see," Guru Mula's voice was still pleasant, "you are now grown to the age when you should be instructed in the way of Islam, and you shall be given a new name that will show everyone that you follow Allah and His prophet."

"I don't want a new name."

"We have planned a great name feast at which you will be honored, and after the name feast, all the people will respect you as the young chief and you will be greatly favored by all of us."

Satoo looked at the circle of faces around him as he rose to leave. "You must all excuse me now," he said. "I shall be late for the singing."

Satoo looked at the circle of faces around him, but Tama could not detect any hesitation or fear in his glance. "You must all excuse me now." He rose to leave. "I shall be late for the singing. I never miss, you know."

"Wait, wait!" The voice of Guru Mula was harsh now and his eyes, no longer smiling, glared at the boy. "You will be sorry for this. Your family have all chosen to follow the prophet. You cannot defy Islam."

"If worshipping God according to His own Holy Book is defiance of Islam, then I defy Islam." Satoo's face did not lose its smile nor his voice its gentleness, but as he hurried down the steps of the ladder it seemed to Tama that he stood straighter and held his head higher, and Tama watched him until he disappeared in the shadows that crept darkly up the hill.

For a moment after Satoo left there was silence in the room. Chief Meradin sat bowed forward as though to comfort some inner pain that tormented him.

Tama himself felt his stomach twist and writhe inside him like a wounded animal. For an instant a big bright thought pushed itself into his mind. Gladness had gone out of this room with Satoo. There was no joy or happiness among the men who sat there on the floor. There was only hate, anger, and evil planning here. For just a moment Tama touched the edge of something so great and joyous that he drew back in alarm.

Then he thought of little Marta, her bright eyes shining with gladness and trust. He thought of the big teacher, who had never spoken an unkind word to anyone in the village. Tama began to wish with his whole heart that he had never thought of bringing Islam teachers to Great Sangir.

The big thought passed, and Tama slumped on his mat. He was caught now, caught in the net he had woven himself. Something more wicked than anything he had ever touched with his strongest charms was building up in this room, and he must listen and accept.

"There is only one thing to do." Guru Mula's voice was smooth again. "After all, the boy can never be chief. He mocks at your authority, both of you." He gave Tama a sharp look. "He leads the village people who follow the red-haired teacher. He is already worse than dead to you. I have a plan."

Then the smooth voice went on to unfold a scheme that made Tama tremble, while Chief Meradin sat there with his head in his hands, as though turned to stone among them.

"You have a number of fishing boats down at the landing, and on quiet nights you sometimes go out to fish. Is it not true? Tomorrow night you will go and take Satoo with you. You will put him ashore at the fire mountain and leave him there."

"No, no!" It was the chief's strangled voice speaking through his hands still pressed to his face.

"Oh, we will not abandon him there. No, this is just to be a lesson to him. There he will see how angry the fire spirits are, and he will understand that unless we come to bring him home, he is lost. Don't you see? I think it might persuade him."

Still Chief Meradin did not uncover his face, and it seemed to Tama that his shoulders sagged and shrank till he looked like a very old man, although the chief was still young.

Again Tama felt such a wave of regret surge through him that he could scarcely restrain himself. Why had he ever thought that the Islam teaching would be a good thing for Great Sangir?

The quiet voice of Guru Mula spoke on. "Think now, all of you, is there any other way? We have beaten him and cursed him. We have done everything to change his mind."

But the boy's mother—" the chief spoke again.

"I have thought of that," Guru Mula said. "You can tell her that the boy fell overboard and you could not find him in the darkness. It does happen, you know— the sharks."

Again a long silence filled the room like a loathsome thing.

At last Guru Mula continued, "I am sure, after thinking it over, that you will all agree. There is no other way, and it is possible that by this means the mountain spirits may be quieted. Is it not true that in years past when the fire spirits raged and thundered your people offered them such sacrifices as this?"

"It is true," Tama whispered.

"You see, although we do not believe in spirits, only in Allah, still we do not change your old customs."

Tama's hands clenched. The writhing inside his stomach was almost too much now. He could see clearly what was at the back of Guru Mula's plan.

But the man went on. "Tomorrow evening we will do this. There will be no trouble in getting Satoo to go along. He loves to fish, especially if you are along." He fixed his fierce dark eyes on Chief Meradin.

"I will not go." The chief sat now with his hands in his lap. He spoke in a low, tired voice. "I do not want to see it. Surely you—"

"All right, you won't be along. Gola will go with me. The two of us will be enough. But this thing must be done secretly. No one must know."

Tama stood up. "I do not agree to this." He spoke out in a loud voice.

"I think you are touched with the big teacher's magic too," Guru Mula scoffed. "It is not necessary for you to agree. The matter is arranged."

The witchman swallowed the exclamation of fury that rose in his throat and left the house. He swung along the new trail that led down the hill. His body was shaken by such rage as he had never felt before. He lifted his eyes to the sky, reddened now by the flaming mountain, and knew that he had reached the bottom of every thing bitter and miserable.

Anger filled him, anger at the big teacher, who had started all this by coming uninvited to Sangir; anger against the people, who had flocked to the new teaching; anger against Satoo, who had defied him and Islam too; anger against Guru Mula and the other Islam teachers who were more cruel than the spirits he invoked with his deadliest witchcraft. And yes, anger against himself, most of all against himself. He had made too many mistakes, terrible mistakes, and now it was too late to undo them.

Now, should he warn Satoo? No, Satoo deserved to be severely punished. Should he warn the big teacher? No, the big teacher was to blame too.

With a fierce battle raging inside him, the witch doctor lay down on his mat and tried to sleep, but he could not. He got out his charms, but his confidence in them was shaken. The big teacher's magic was stronger than his most powerful charm. Dawn was flushing the sky with a whiter light than the volcano's glow when Tama finally slept.

And the witch doctor dreamed. He dreamed that he stood alone on the strip of white sand at the base of the fire mountain, and the flame roared above him and the ground quaked beneath him, and the voices of the deep places in the roots of the sea thundered in his ears. And then he saw a little white boat bumping the shore where gentle ripples pushed it against the sand. Marta stood in the boat, but she held no paddle in her hand. She held out her arms to him as she had on that day she was lost in the jungle. In his dream he ran to the white boat and climbed in. Then a splendid brightness enfolded him and perfect peace filled his heart. He woke and saw that the sun was high in the heavens. It must be almost noon.

He moved about the hut with such lightness that he felt he must be half flying, so relieved he was from the dark burdens of the night. He went to the spring and bathed, although it seemed almost improper to be bathing at this time of the day. He felt hungry, and cooked a good meal and ate it with such a light heart that often, as he ate, he stopped and laughed aloud to himself.

Now he knew what he must do. First of all he must find Marta. It might be that the little child had something important to show him or tell him, something that must be important for him to follow. The witchman never doubted that the dream meant something good. He had never in his life known such gladness, such peace. Could this brightness of peace be the God that the big teacher worshipped? All at once he knew that he had changed, and like Satoo, he would never be turned back, no, not for anything.

On the beach not far from the big teacher's house, Tama found Hans and Marta sitting in the shade of a coral rock. They were building a village in the sand. Every few minutes Marta ran out to bring in a shell or a bit of seaweed to arrange the village according to her plan.

Tama squatted down on the beach beside the children.

"Where is your friend, the chief's son?"

"He went fishing with Gola and Guru Mula." Hans placed a stone carefully in the sand village—a stone with a steep, rough angle that looked like a hut with a steep roof. "They intended to go tonight, but the sea is calm today and the Islam teacher said he knew where to look for fish in the daytime."

Hans stood up and pointed to the horizon where a black speck bobbed far out beyond the fire mountain. "He will be back before we sing tonight. He never misses, you know."

Chapter Ten

SATOO'S VICTORY

When Satoo left the house of Guru Mula and ran down the hill toward the big teacher's house on the sand, he found a question rising in his mind. He sat down be side the path to think it over. This was to have been a council to arrange some way of driving the teacher away from Great Sangir, but it hadn't turned out that way. At least he had heard nothing of that sort. The whole object of the meeting seemed to center on forcing him, the chief's son, to forsake the teaching of the Holy Book and follow Islam.

Perhaps they would discuss other things after he left, but he lifted his eyes to the house on the hill and saw Tama coming out the door, his figure silhouetted against the light inside Guru Mula's house. Without Tama, Satoo knew that the others would not make any important decision.

He knew that his father, the chief, held the witch doctor's opinions in great regard. Also he feared Tama's medicine. Chief Meradin wouldn't act on anything without advice from his witchman.

Satoo didn't want to see Tama just now, and he would certainly take this trail down the hill. The boy leaped up and ran again until he came to the teacher's house. There he went in and took his place among the other worshipers, who sat on mats in the large room.

On this evening the big teacher taught them a grand new hymn. He explained to them that a great and good man had written both the words and the music more than three hundred years ago, but the magic in it was strong, and right now the Christians on the island of Sangir needed the power of this song. The words began:

Satoo felt a huge hand laid on him. Then a loud voice shouted in his ears above the thunder of the mountain. It was the voice of the teacher.

"A mighty mountain is our God,

A wall that will not falter."

Satoo reached for the majestic notes and the powerful words along with all the others. The teacher's voice led them, and the hymn filled the night. Satoo felt his fears and doubts dissolve in the safety and assurance of the holy magic.

After the meeting ended, the power of the song was still strong on him. The village people filed out the door, and Hans whispered to him, "Did they make a plan?"

"No, no plan," Satoo smiled. "No plan at all. The only thing they did was try to persuade me to follow Islam."

The big teacher came and laid a hand on each boy's shoulder. "Satoo, there may be more heavy trials for you," he said. "Do not be afraid. God will hear your prayers and your songs and He will save you for His kingdom. The thing you must do now is to be kind to all of them. God is a God of love, not of fear or anger."

Satoo ran home. He paused a moment in front of Tama's hut. He could see the faint glimmer of the oil lamp under the closed door. He would like to know what Tama thought about the words spoken in Guru Mula's house. He remembered the look on the witchman's face.

He hesitated for a moment only, thinking perhaps he should go in and tell Tama about the powerful new song and his own great joy and peace. He remembered what the big teacher had said, "God is pulling on Tama's heart.

He decided not to go in. It was already late and his father was sure to be angry. He hurried on home, crept into the house, surprised to find no one awake. In the dark he found his sleeping mat and lay down to sleep.

In the night a sound aroused him. He raised up on his elbow. It had sounded like a man sobbing. He listened for a long time, but the sound did not come again, and Satoo felt sure now that he must have dreamed it. He lay down and went fast asleep. When he wakened the morning had come.

After he had bathed and eaten and finished the tasks his mother required of him, he ran down to the beach. It was already midmorning, and he found Hans busy making a sand village for Marta. He squatted down in the shade of the big coral rock where they played and began to help arrange the sticks and shells and seaweed that Marta brought them.

Old Gola came along the beach with his fish nets hung over his shoulder. He was headed for his fishing boat that lay with the others at the landing place."

Why do you go to fish in the middle of the day?" Satoo asked the old man.

"We did plan to go this evening," Gola answered, "but we have decided to go while the sun is high, because Guru Mula has told me that far out in the sea, on a calm day like this, we may find big gatherings of the flat fish; you know, those speckled ones that taste better than any others."

Satoo put down the stones and shells he was arranging. He was always eager to hear about new fish or new ways of catching fish. He listened to Gola's words.

"See," Gola pointed. "Guru Mula will come with me to show us how to find the fish and catch them."

Satoo looked up to the Islam teachers' houses on the hill. He saw Guru Mula coming down the path.

"Why don't you come with us?" Gola asked Satoo.

"I'd have to ask my father."

"I have already asked him and he doesn't care. He said you may go if you like."

Satoo looked at his friend. "Will you let Hans go too?"

"No, I think we'll have a full load with you. This boat isn't very big, and we may catch a lot of fish." Gola turned toward the boat.

Satoo stood and looked at Hans for a moment, trying to make up his mind. Neither Gola nor Guru Mula had been very pleasant last night, but he remembered what the big teacher had said about being kind to all of them. He could play with Hans any day, and he didn't get a chance to go fishing often. This was special, too, going clear out to sea, and in daytime. He hoped they really would find some of the delicious flat fish. He ran after Gola and climbed into the fishing boat.

"I will be back for the singing tonight," he called back to Hans in a loud voice. His friend stood up and waved. Satoo was sure he had heard and understood him.

Gola loosened the rattan thong that tied the boat, and they pushed out into the ocean. The sea was quite calm and the surface moved in long swells that never broke, and tiny ripples flashed along the green water. It was a perfect day for sailing. Although the breeze was so gentle there was enough of it to fill the bark-cloth sail, and it pulled them along at an easy roll. They must pass directly between the point of high rocks where Satoo had his secret lookout perch and the white sandy strip of beach along the southern base of the volcano.

From here both places looked very close. The smoking mouth of the fire mountain opened on the opposite, or northern, side, and the flow of molten rock streamed down that slope so the volcano did not look so frightening from here. The noise of the thundering was louder. The mountain towered over the tiny boat and the bursting and hissing noises sounded much too close. The sharp smell of its breath made him cough and shudder. He was glad they didn't have to go any closer.

Out in the sea they hunted for fish, and, sure enough, just as Guru Mula had promised, they did find gatherings of the flat fish. The two men threw the nets again and again and drew in scores of them. Satoo helped with the work, and by evening there was a fine catch of fish aboard old Gola's boat.

Satoo was hungry. He knew how delicious those fish would taste baked over the coals in his mother's clay stove. He settled back in the boat, and the two men pulled toward home. The boy closed his eyes and dozed a little. Then he woke with a start. The sail was down and both men bent over the paddles.

He saw that Guru Mula, who guided the boat, was steering straight for the southern side of the fire mountain.

"Why do you swing in so close?" he asked.

Guru Mula didn't answer. His face was set and stern.

Satoo turned to Gola. "Isn't it dangerous to run so close to the fire mountain?"

Gola answered nothing. Now they were but a short distance from the curve of white sandy beach that lay like a thin, waning moon between two of the southern buttresses of the mountain in the sea.

The roar of continuing thunder, the hiss of water, and the sound of bursting flame drowned out all other noises. It was now impossible to shout loud enough to make anyone hear anything, and the boat lurched forward, hard onto the firm white sand. As it struck, Satoo felt himself lifted in strong arms and tossed out into the shallow water near the beach. Before he could scramble to his feet or utter a cry of protest, Gola's boat was shoved off and was making for the landing place on Great Sangir, right in front of the teacher's house.

Satoo crawled out of the water onto the beach and stood there on the narrow strip of sand too stunned for words. He looked after the boat. It was too far off to be overtaken, and now Gola hoisted the sail and it skimmed away on the land breeze. When Satoo recovered enough to scream out his terror, there was not a living thing to hear. And the thunder of the mountain mocked him.

He sat down on the sand. The ground quaked beneath him. Deep undertones and overtones of thunder rumbled beneath the mountain and the sea. Even here the glow of flame that belched from the northern side and blistered the opposite slope of the volcano cast a faint red glow through the gathering night.

He thought of throwing himself into the sea, but that would do no good. He could only drown, fine swimmer that he was and the sharks might not let him do that. He had seen plenty of sharks this day. Never had he faced such terror before.

Why had they done it? He remembered Guru Mula's stern face and cruel eyes. He remembered something he had said last night about defying Islam. He couldn't even remember that the Guru had finished the sentence. They must have planned it after he left. Of course his father didn't know—or did he?

He doubted whether Tama knew. So this was the way men of Islam punished those who would not follow their commands. He shuddered again. So fierce the mountain raged, so wild the noises and the rocking thunder that Satoo found it almost impossible to think, but he must think.

Now, what would the big teacher do in such a circumstance as this? He would sing of course. Satoo opened his mouth and tried to sing, but no song could come out in this tempest of flame and noise. In his mind he did remember the words of the new song the teacher had taught them last night:

"A mighty mountain is our God,

A wall that will not falter."

Now what kind of mountain could be more mighty than this volcano? Was God a greater mountain than this?

"A mighty mountain is our God."

The words swept through his mind like a strong wind that cooled and quieted him. He remembered many things the big teacher had taught them from the Holy Book of God's magic, but none of them swelled in his heart so near and so powerful as the song.

Then Satoo thought of Hans. Hans would expect him back for evening worship. Would Hans see the fishing boat come in to the landing? Would he run out to welcome him and find that he was not there? Hans would surely tell his father. Hans would surely tell, and the big teacher would do something—surely he would do something. He shut his eyes and tried to see the teacher's white boat tied among the others at the landing.

Then a dreadful thought struck him. The men would never admit that they had thrown him ashore on the fire mountain. They would invent some lie. They would say he had fallen overboard and drowned. If Hans believed...if the big teacher believed...if father and mother believed, then none of them would do anything at all, because it would be too late. They would all feel sorry, and in time they would forget.

Slowly the full meaning of his situation became clear to him. He was here on the fire mountain without food or water. True, the jungle grew on the lower slopes of the volcano on this side, but no animal could live here. He remembered that even the birds no longer came. Back in his mind a memory stirred of something he had heard from his father, something he had told Hans that long ago the men of Sangir had offered living sacrifices, men, women, and children, to the spirits of the volcano.

Night blackened the whole world, but the volcano raged and shook like a living thing, and the boy who cowered on the narrow crescent of white sand looked across the water toward the shore and saw a light flicker on the beach. That would be the light in the big teacher's house. They must be gathering now to sing the songs. They would sing the new song again tonight

"A mighty mountain is our God."

Then Satoo threw himself on the sand and lay with his face to the damp beach. It seemed to him that the acrid fumes of the mountain's breath were not so strong here. And Satoo prayed. He had prayed often before, since Hans taught him, but now that he was all alone on this fearful mountain, the words burst from his heart, and he cried out to the God of heaven, not for help from the shore. He had given up all hope of that, but for strength to endure, for perfect trust and the power to sing out in his heart the honor and praise of the God he had chosen to worship.

A convulsion of unusual violence shook the strip of sand where he lay, and under his outstretched hands the earth opened. A hissing, gushing noise filled his ears and the hot breath of fire blasted into his face. He drew back from the abyss.

Then he felt a huge hand laid on him, and a loud voice shouted in his ear above the thunder of the mountain. It was the voice of the teacher.

Chapter Eleven

THE FIRE MOUNTAIN

It was late in the night, and the big teacher pulled his boat through the calm water toward the light that shone from the door and windows of his own home on the sand. Satoo lay in the bow of the boat with his head on a roll of fish nets where the teacher had put him.

"Rest, now," the deep, kind voice had said. "This has been a frightening day, a terrible experience for you. Don't talk; don't look back; just rest."

It was easy for Satoo to rest. He didn't even need to open his eyes to know that the big teacher sat there before him with a paddle in each hand, and he knew that every stroke of those powerful arms brought them nearer home...home? He wondered whether there would ever be a home for him again within his father's house.

The noises of the volcano receded into the distance and the thunderings sounded far away to Satoo's ears as the teacher brought the boat alongside the wharf. He raised up then, and he saw at once that never before had the mountain behaved in so wild a manner. He knew now why the teacher had told him not to look backward.

Surely no living person on Sangir would sleep this night, not with that monster blowing out sheets of flame and shattering all the earth with thunder.

Even before the teacher picked up the rattan thong to fasten the boat, Hans scrambled aboard. He must have been waiting and watching here.

"You were there! You were there! I knew it, I knew it! " He threw his arms about his friend and dragged him from the boat. Satoo still shook a little and felt weak, but he had begun to feel much better.

The two boys stood together on the wharf and looked out toward the fire mountain. Although it was deep night and a peculiar murky quality dimmed the air about them, Satoo could see that something had happened to the fire mountain.

He clutched Hans's arm. "Look! It has sunk. The fire is coming out of the sea!"

"Wait," Hans said. "Wait."

Then Satoo saw that flames gushed from two places, one far up at the mountain's summit and another down near the surface of the ocean.

"It has been like that since sundown," Hans told him.

The island boy felt his body tremble. "And the big teacher...he knew? He saw that? And yet he came for me?"

Now Hans's mother ran out of the house on the sand with Marta in her arms. The big teacher took the little girl and comforted her against his breast, for she was crying with fear at the sight of the mountain and the unnatural heaving of the earth. With his arm around his wife the big man turned to the boys.

"You will stay here with us tonight, Satoo. I'm sure no one in the village expects you home. It might even be dangerous for Guru Mula to see you."

With a surge of sharp sadness Satoo answered, "I will stay."

After the teacher and his wife had taken little Marta to the house, Hans and Satoo still stood watching the volcano. Satoo could not forget that just a short time ago he had been there on the fire mountain, with the awful crack opening under his hands and the fire and noise and the smell of brimstone in his face. Then his mind came back to here and now. He realized that Hans was talking to him.

"Your father wouldn't let any of the Christian people go to the hills," Hans said.

"Have the village people gone to the hills?"

Yes, most of them went this afternoon. Tama went with them. Only the Islam teachers and a few of the village people are up here on the hill back of us.

"Where are the Christian people now?"

"They are at their homes in the village. My father told them to go home and try to rest, and to come back if the mountain got worse before morning."

The teacher's wife laid mats on the floor of the big room and told the two boys they might sleep there, but both of them were too excited to sleep, and in the end they sat outside on the salt grass and watched the volcano.

"How did you know where I was?" Satoo asked Hans.

"Well, I felt sorry because Gola wouldn't let me go along to fish, and I didn't feel like playing at the sand village any more. I took Marta in, and after we had eaten and she was asleep I climbed up to our perch in the rocks. I thought about what you had told me of the meeting they had in Guru Mula's house last night and how they were trying to force you to follow Islam. Then I began to feel afraid."

"Could you see Gola's boat from up there?"

"Oh, yes. It was just a little speck out there, but I could see it hang there like a black dot on the horizon. I looked at the volcano too, and it seemed to be acting worse than we had ever seen it before."

"Did you stay there the rest of the day?"

"No. After I had watched the boat and the mountain for a while I saw that something was going on over at the village. People were packing their cooking pots and rolling their mats. Then I saw them climbing up the path to the hills. I came down then, because I thought if they were going to go up to the high land maybe we should go too."

"Why did you decide not to go?"

"The Christian people all came over to our house. They said that the chief had told them to go to the big teacher for protection, that the fire spirits were about to destroy the house on the sand."

"Weren't you all afraid?"

"Oh, yes, I suppose so, but my father had them all stay, and we sang and prayed and sang some more, and now they have gone back to their houses to sleep."

"They won't sleep this night," Satoo said as he watched the volcano. "I still don't know how you found out that I was out there."

"Toward evening," Hans went on with his story, "when I thought the fishing boat was about to return I climbed back up to the rocks to see if it was coming. I saw it all right, not far from the fire mountain. I couldn't understand why they pulled in so close to the volcano. It looked to me as if they paddled directly toward it. When I saw the boat touch the beach—you know, the place where we saw the big bird—I knew something bad had happened. It was just sundown, but after the boat came on toward the landing here, I thought I could see something on the sand. It looked a little like that big bird we watched, but I was sure it must be you."

"Did you meet the boat when Gola and Guru Mula came back?"

"Yes. I ran down from the rocks and I waited for them here. I'm sure they expected me to be here. They both looked very sad and said they had bad news for the chief; that you had stood up in the boat to help haul in a net and had fallen into the sea. Gola told of how they tried to get you out, but your body was all tangled up with the net, and while they worked to get you loose a shark came up..."

"And then...?"

"And then I ran back to our house, shouting in our own language to my father. I told him that they had put you on the volcano. Of course they must have heard me shout, but I suppose they thought I shouted from fright because of what had happened to you."

"And then the new mouth of fire opened on the volcano?"

"It had already opened before the men got to shore. They saw it. I think they were frightened, but they did not leave the fish. They took it all up to the Islam teachers' houses. It took several trips, and the other men came down and helped them."

Hans explained to Satoo how all the Christian people had come out to see the new mouth of fire in the volcano, but the big teacher did not tell anyone that Satoo was out on the mountain. Of course none of the village people knew that Satoo had gone with Gola, and the day had been full of terror and excitement. Before the men had finished unloading the fish, the teacher had sent the Christian people home.

"And then he came out after me?"

"Yes; as soon as they finished with the fish my father got ready to go. I wanted to go with him, but he said the volcano looked so threatening that he would rather I didn't go. So I waited here. It was a long time."

"Hans, it is the God of heaven who saved me. The song is true."

"What do you mean?"

" 'A mighty mountain is our God,

A wall that will not falter.' "

Flames from the fire mountain still flashed across the sky, and the earth trembled and thunder rolled and echoed beneath them. The two boys sat close together on the salt grass close to the house on the sand, and after a while the big teacher came and sat with them.

All along the high peaks of the inland hills tiny lights flickered and winked into the murky night—campfires of terrified people who had fled from the fury of the volcano.

"Maybe we should go up there too," Hans said.

"No," the teacher said. "No; I have thought about it and we have prayed about it all afternoon. Of course we could go, but it would mean a fight on the trail, because the chief forbade any of the Christian people to leave the village. He thinks the fire spirits are angry and intend to destroy us. This is a time for us to stand still and see what God will do for us."

"What about Satoo?" Hans asked.

"Of course no one knows where Satoo is. That is another good reason for us to stay here in our own house. We can hide him here. Guru Mula would stop at nothing now."

It was past midnight, and they all went into the house and lay down, but the trembling of the earth and the noise of thunder kept them awake. Before dawn all the Christian people came back. None of them had slept. All of them seemed to gather courage from the big teacher's strong faith and his songs of praise.

When Tama heard from Hans that Gola's fishing boat had already gone out into the sea and that Satoo had gone along, all his terrible sadness came back. He crouched on the log wharf for a few minutes, looking at the tiny speck that was Gola's fishing boat. He knew that Guru Mula had not waited until evening because he had feared that Chief Meradin would interfere, that in the end he would not allow his son to be taken to the volcano.

Again a tempest of anger swept the witchman's mind and soul. But this time his fury was directed at Guru Mula. He must go at once and tell the chief. Without doubt Chief Meradin thought Satoo was playing on the beach with the big teacher's children.

Before Tama got back to the village he saw that the villagers were preparing to leave. He hurried to the chief's house and told him what had happened. The chief looked at him, but his eyes were dull as dark pebbles under murky water, and he spoke sternly. "Let him be. Do you not see how angry the fire spirits are? The village people are all too frightened to stay here. We must go to the hills. It must certainly be because of my son that they are so angry."

Tama helped the people pack up their things, and as they set out on the trail one of the Christian men asked if they might also go along.

"No, you may not go. You have chosen to follow the big teacher. Now go and tell him that you are afraid. Go sing your songs and pray your prayers, but don't let me catch any of you on the hill trail and don't try to cut your way up through the jungle either. I have set Guru Mula to watch and see that not a single Christian goes anywhere but to the house on the beach."

Tama could see that the chief raged with anger and terrible sorrow. He decided to say nothing more. Twice he made the journey up to the central ridge of hills, and it was after midnight when he finally came back to the village. He knew that no one remained now but the Christians. He looked at the fire mountain. It belched forth more fire. A new mouth had opened. The thunderings were louder, the quakings the worst in his memory, and Satoo was out there. What must it be like—out there?

Tama went down to the beach. He looked toward the teacher's house. There was no light. He could not think that they were asleep, but at least they were inside the house. Perhaps they would not see him. Any how he didn't care. He bent to untie his own boat. With trembling hands he reached for his paddle. Then a dark form loomed beside him.

"Ah, Chief Meradin, does your thought go with mine?"

"My thought goes with yours," the chief said in a low, choked voice.

He looked at the volcano, and his whole body shook. He could scarcely speak. "It is dreadful...terrible...I guess they are angry at me. Satoo is out there. Gola told me."

The men settled themselves in the boat and pushed off. They were halfway to the volcano before they spoke again. Then the chief said, "Satoo will expect me. He will know that I must come."

Now the men could no longer talk. The raging of the mountain forbade. Tama guided the boat and made for the only possible landing on the southern side—the strip of sandy beach.

Had it been possible, Tama would have turned back. The mountain now raged at him like a living creature. The fire and smoke and hot blasts of foul air, the cracking thunder that tore through depths of ocean and land, seemed directed at him alone. Was he not the medicine man of this village? Was he not the witchman who had controlled the spirits and powers of evil?

Now Tama felt that he had been mistaken all along about the reason for the fire spirits' anger. It must have been at about the time Satoo was thrown on the volcano that the new mouth of flame had opened.

Now they were almost upon the beach. Flames reddened the sky and showed the sand as bare as the top of a rock. No person was there. Tama would have sworn that he had already tasted the dregs of everything terrible and grievous, but this...this was worse.

The chief threw himself upon the sand. Then Tama saw the crack that opened down to the water's edge. Even as he watched, a breath of stench belched up from the wide crack, terrible thunder spoke from the depths, and the sea boiled up in it like a sizzling rice pot.

Tama dragged the chief to the boat and paddled back to the shore without a word.

"I will go to the hills," the chief said, after they had tied the boat. "I can get to my people before morning."

"I will go to Guru Mula's house. I will see if I can find out anything we don't already know."

The chief waved this aside with a gesture of complete hopelessness. "It is no use... no use at all. But do you think it is quite safe at the Islam teacher's house?"

"Oh, yes, it is probably safe, as safe as anything on this side of the island."

The men parted, and Tama hurried up the new trail to Guru Mula's house.

By the time the sun rose and looked down on Sangir everything on the southwest side of the island had changed. The village was deserted. All the Christian people were gathered in the garden at the big teacher's house. The chief and the other villagers had fled to the high ridge of hills, because they could no longer bear the thundering of the fire mountain and the shaking earth. The air hung heavy with doom. The smell of brimstone choked everyone, and above it all the sun shone down with terrible heat. Only above the volcano clouds hung dark. Fierce lightning shot through them and tore them apart to show bursting flames.

From the house of Guru Mula, Tama looked down on the group of Christians gathered within the little garden of the house on the sand.

"You know they are in great danger there," Guru Mula said. "A big wave from that mountain would sweep them away like a handful of sand."

"Yes, I guess it would." Tama's hammering heart felt as if it had swollen to fill his chest. He was thinking of little Marta. He could see her dancing around among the people like a butterfly.

Then Tama heard the voice of the big teacher raised in song. The melody rose and fell in the troubled air. It swelled and died away, and rose again and again, as though in answer to the thunder of the volcano. The teacher must have translated the words of the song into the island language, for Tama could understand.

"A mighty mountain is our God,

A wall that will not falter."

What could such words mean? God...a mountain? Then the thought of Satoo pushed into his tormented mind. He trembled to think of what the boy must have suffered there on the fire mountain—before what?

He faced it at last—before that hideous crack on the beach of the volcano swallowed him up.

Chapter Twelve

GOD'S VICTORY

As Tama looked down from the Islam teacher's garden over the house on the sand where the big red-haired teacher lived, he could make out, even from here, the stone-trough garden of green leaves and red blossoms and the neat walled-in yard. All morning he had watched the fierce anger of the fire mountain. Yet even above the thunder the sound of singing wafted up to him as the Christians in the teacher's garden sang the terrible day away.

Something drew him toward the house on the sand, but he resisted. A couple of days before he had been sure that he would follow the God of heaven. Now his mind filled with doubt and his heart ached with sadness.

The sun had passed midheaven now, but there was no slackening of the volcano's fury. Something terrible threatened. Sweat stood out on Tama's body, yet he shivered with cold. He could not get Satoo out of his mind. He was sure, now, that the boy had fallen into the wide crack on the beach at the fire mountain's base.

The fire spirits cared nothing that he and the chief had risked their lives to undo the wrong. The fire spirits cared nothing that he would give his own life gladly could he see the chief's son well and happy as he had been that night in Guru Mula's house.

Then Tama remembered his dream of little Marta in the white boat and how he had gotten into the boat and found himself so peaceful and happy that he had wakened from joy. Then all that newborn happiness was shattered by Gola and Guru Mula when they—he refused to think about it. Marta, Marta, he could still see her among those singing people down there on the sand.

Tama shook with fear and weakness. The dreadful thing that hung over the land could be felt. For two days no one had eaten. No one had slept. Each moment the awful thing they waited for drew nearer, yet no one could say what threatened or when it would arise and devour them. The heaving, writhing volcano just off the southwestern shore of Great Sangir was like a gigantic animal dying in agony yet roaring and thundering and reaching in its torment to pull everything and everyone after it.

The mouth of lowest hell had opened and sucked with its awful breath at every living thing. Only the blue ocean lapping round the mountain's base looked peaceful, and the tempest in Tama's mind threatened greater calamity than the fire mountain.

No one could stay inside the houses. All the Islam teachers and the Islam worshipers who had gathered there stood among the fruit trees on the hill in front of their buildings and looked at the mountain, turning often to search one another's face for a shred of comfort or hope. They looked with scorn on the little group of praying Christians in the big teacher's garden. Tama, alone of the whole group, tried to weigh the danger and hope that nothing bad would happen to little Marta.

"It's a good thing the chief left me here to see that those Christians don't get away," Guru Mula said. "If we weren't out here watching I should expect them to bolt for the hills any minute."

The thunder under the ground rose in a tremendous roar. Every face grew pale. Both mouths of the volcano spewed forth a sickening blast of fiery rock. At the same instant the solid earth of the mountain sprang apart. Tama saw the whole northern half of the volcano explode into the sky and settle with a crashing hiss into the sea.

Then Tama flashed down the hill like a winged creature. He heard shouts of the Islam people behind him as they urged him back, but he only ran faster.

Even as he ran he saw the ocean sucked back almost to the roots of the volcano. Then a mighty wall of water piled higher and higher and rolled toward the shore.

There was only one thought in Tama's mind—to save Marta. He strained toward the beach like a maddened creature. He leaped the low rock wall that shut in the teacher's garden. He saw Marta in the midst of the singing people, and the sound of the powerful song filled his ears.

"Run! Run!" he gasped with his last breath. Couldn't they hear? Couldn't they understand? Oh, what madness!

He grabbed Marta and clutched her to him. He turned to the low rock wall. Could he make it back up the hill to safety?

No, it was too late. The big teacher laid a heavy hand on the witchman's shoulder and drew him into the midst of the group of singing people, just as the enormous wave broke with deafening thunder on the beach in front of the little house on the sand.

Even as the wave struck, the words of the song lifted about him:

" 'A mighty mountain is our God,

A wall that will not falter.' "

Tama shut his eyes and clutched the child in terror. Thunder crashed overhead, and then he looked.

"The wall!" he cried "The wall that will not falter!"

The mountainous wave had divided just below the gate of the big teacher's garden and passed by on both sides outside the low rock fence. It stood up to heaven, surely the height of three palm trees, a green wall filled with fishing boats and huge driftwood logs, strange deep sea creatures, shells, and snarled tangles of seaweed.

The wave united into one just back of the teacher's garden, and Tama couldn't see how far it washed up the hill. In an instant it surged back into the ocean, and when the following wave came it reached only to the front gate of the garden.

Tama still held Marta in his arms, but weakness overcame him now and he sank to the salt grass and closed his eyes. Then Satoo bent over him.

"Ah, Tama, God has saved you." The boy's voice broke with gladness. "God lifted up His wall and saved us all."

Tama opened his eyes. In a burst of wonder he sat up. "How came you here? You? Satoo?" He looked about him, knowing that he must have completely lost his mind. "What magic is this?"

Then all the Christian people gathered around him. Tama could see that they regarded his presence among them as a miracle equal to the miracle of the divided water. They looked upon him with love, and as they sang and praised God for the mighty deliverance, Tama knelt with them.

Later he sat on the salt grass with Marta beside him. Satoo came over to speak to him again. "Gola and Guru Mula planned to harm me, you know; but our God is a mighty mountain, just as the song says. He is a mighty wall, too, as you have seen."

All around the big teacher's garden the wreckage of the giant tidal wave was piled high, much higher than the whitewashed rock wall. Driftwood, seaweed, deep sea shells, and broken pieces of the houses from the slope of the hill mingled with sand, rocks, dead sea animals, and scraps of fishing boats. When they went to look, there were no houses left in the village, but most of the coconut palms still stood. Nothing remained of the Islam teachers' houses and garden. Only the people who had fled to the high hills in the middle of the island survived. Those and the little group of Christians who sang and prayed inside the teacher's low rock wall.

Early the next day the village people came straggling back from the hills, but Tama and Satoo had al- ready climbed the trail. They saw the chief round the bend in the path where he could see the destruction of the sea. He stood there like a man whose life had ended, although his body still stood upright and moved.

"My father, my father." Satoo ran to him, and the chief's arms went round him with questioning wonder.

"My son, my son—but my son is dead!" He looked with wild eyes at Tama, who tried to explain.

The big teacher went out and brought him in. That was why we didn't find him. He has been at the teacher's house since then."

"The Islam teachers?"

"Swept away. Nothing left of them or their houses."

"But you were with them, Tama." Again the wild look came into Chief Meradin's eyes as though he thought himself mad, and this a strange new world he had never seen before.

"Yes, I was with them. But I thought in my heart to save little Marta. I saw the mountain blow to pieces, and I knew the big wave must come. I ran down to the teacher's house. I grabbed Marta and would have run back, but the big teacher caught me and pulled me back among the singing people. Come, come and see!" Tama's voice broke with joy and wonder.

When the chief had seen all, when he understood how the great wave had divided and destroyed every thing, even the Islam teachers' houses on the higher slope, he sat down on the beach for a day and a night and spoke not one word to anyone.

When he rose up again he called all the people who remained of his village and all the people from other parts of the island to see the miracle that the God of heaven had done. He told the story of how Guru Mula had put Satoo on the fire mountain and how the big teacher had rescued him. He pointed to the bare and ruined slope where the Islam teachers' fine new houses had stood.

"Listen to me," he said. "This mountain and this wave were controlled by the God these people worship. The Islam teachers are swept away and so is Gola. Tama is here because he loved the big teacher's little girl."

He raised his voice and spoke with strong words. "This is the true magic. In all the world there is no God like the big teacher's God, who is able to deliver him from the anger of the fire mountain and the great wave. So I make a proclamation that from this day we must follow this magic and our children will follow after us. I, Chief Meradin, have spoken."

He sat down, and all the people said Ah-h-h-h-h." For they all knew of the great thing that had happened, and they feared God and honored the big teacher.

No one was surprised that Tama became the teacher's helper from that very day and was stronger for God than he had ever been for the old witchcraft.

Now, although the people camped outside under bits of mat and shelters of branches, they met every night in the teacher's house. There was not room for them, and there was not even room in the garden. Many of the young ones climbed the huge pile of drift that rose above the rock wall. Now, when they looked to the sea and the fire mountain there was no thunder and no flame. There was no quiver of the earth, for peace had settled over Sangir, and all was quiet.

When the chief suggested that the whole village help clear away the pile of drift the tidal wave had deposited about the teacher's garden, the teacher objected.

"No, I want this to stay just as it is," he said. "You see how huge and wide it is. Even if all of us worked every day, it would take many days to move it. Let it stand, so that everyone may remember what God has done."

The chief talked of moving the village away from the spot where it formerly stood, but the big teacher advised them to build everything as it had been before but with better houses and more neatness. He and Hans helped them, and everyone worked together. Before many weeks a fine new village stood where it had been before. The village spring and the jungle springs still flowed with clear fresh water, and over the burned-out fire mountain the ocean's green water lay smooth and deep, deep as the peace that had come to Sangir, deep as the everlasting mercy of God.

Years afterward, when Satoo was chief of the village and Tama an aged man, scientists came from Europe to see the spot where the tidal wave had divided. These men from the big cities did not believe that such a thing had really happened, but when they saw the drift that remained they knew that this story was true. The God who divided the Red Sea and the Jordan River is the same yesterday, today, and forever. He is still able to lead His people to victory through songs of praise even as He did the armies of King Jehoshaphat in ancient times.

For us, even today:

> "A mighty mountain is our God,
>
> A wall that will not falter."

We invite you to view the complete
selection of titles we publish at:
www.TEACHServices.com

scan with your mobile
device to go directly
to our website

Please write or email us your praises, reactions, or
thoughts about this or any other book we publish at:

TEACH Services, Inc.
PUBLISHING
www.TEACHServices.com ● (800) 367-1844

P.O. Box 954
Ringgold, GA 30736

Info@TEACHServices.com

TEACH Services, Inc., titles may be purchased in bulk
for educational, business, fund-raising, or sales
promotional use. For information, please e-mail:

BulkSales@TEACHServices.com

Finally if you are interested in seeing
your own book in print, please contact us at

publishing@TEACHServices.com

We would be happy to review your manuscript for free.

www.ingramcontent.com/pod-product-compliance
Lightning Source LLC
Chambersburg PA
CBHW060546100426
42742CB00013B/2472